Grand Prix
Championship Courses
and Drivers

BOOKS BY GRIFFITH BORGESON

The Golden Age of the American Racing Car
Grand Prix Championship Courses and Drivers

Grand Prix Championship Courses and Drivers

by Griffith Borgeson

Illustrated with photographs and diagrams

W · W · NORTON & COMPANY · INC ·
New York

Copyright © 1968 by W. W. Norton & Company, Inc.
First Edition
Library of Congress Catalog Card No. 68-22718
All Rights Reserved
Published simultaneously in Canada by
George J. McLeod Limited, Toronto
Printed in the United States of America

1 2 3 4 5 6 7 8 9 0

For Hubert Schroeder, distinguished servant of the sport and incomparable friend; and to the memory of Jim Clark, champion of champions, who lost his life on the Hockenheim Circuit in Germany on April 7, 1968.

Contents

Introduction

International Grand Prix racing was created in 1900 by a wealthy American in Paris, which then was the automotive capital of the world. The man was James Gordon Bennett, owner and publisher of the *New York Herald Tribune* and its Paris edition. He foresaw the automobile's fantastic future and chose racing as a way to hasten its progress.

Remarkably enough, it was not until fifty years later that the automotive sport's international governing body established a scoring system by means of which the champion racing driver of the world could be selected each year. The World Championship of Drivers breathed new meaning, new human interest, and new excitement into Grand Prix racing, which, throughout its history, has been an ultimate test of man and machine.

This book is a guide to this greatest of motor-racing championships, to the arenas in which they are contested, and to the men who have attained its most lofty heights.

I

Inside Grand Prix Racing

Inside Grand Prix Racing

The first motor race to bear the title of Grand Prix, meaning "grand prize," was organized by the Automobile Club of France (ACF) in 1906. It replaced the annual Gordon Bennett Cup Races but carried on the tradition of competition between nations as well as between drivers and between makes, which the Gordon Bennett races had fostered.

The Grand Prix of the ACF immediately became the world's first-ranked automobile speed contest and was soon imitated in other countries. In common with all major sports, this one required organization, control, and impartial regulation, particularly on the international level. These were provided by the Paris-based International Association of Recognized Automobile Clubs (AIACR) and its International Sporting Commission (CSI). As certain speed contests outside of France also grew to major status, they came to be recognized by the AIACR as Grandes Epreuves, or "great tests," "trials," or "proofs." In English these most important of Grands Prix are officially termed the Classic Events and, unofficially, the Epic Events.

Following World War II the AIACR was reorganized and its name was changed to the International Automobile Federation (FIA). Its duties remained the same: coordinating the sport and making and enforcing the regulations which govern it. The CSI of the FIA continued to be thoroughly international, composed of delegates from the national automobile clubs of many nations. It is composed today of representatives of the sport from Austria, Belgium, France, Great Britain, Italy, Mexico, Monaco, Spain, Sweden, the United States of America, Union of Soviet Socialist Republics, and West Germany.

One of the duties of the CSI is to define the "formulae," the funda-

3

mental rules, governing each branch of the sport. These rules usually deal with such basics as engine size and car weight. They are revised every few years in the light of what seems to be in the best interest of the sport. The rules governing Grand Prix machinery are known as Formula One. For the seasons 1966 through 1970 they permitted a maximum engine size of 3 liters and a minimum weight of 1102 pounds.

In 1949, the Italian delegate Marquis Antonio Brivio Sforza, a brilliant driver in his own right, made a historic proposal to the CSI. He suggested a World Championship of Drivers, the championship to be awarded to the driver winning the greatest number of Grandes Epreuves in a given year. The idea received the approval of all delegates and has been in effect since the beginning of the 1950 Grand Prix season. The method of distributing points has been refined over the years, and until the 1967 season the championship was calculated on the following points system:

PLACE	POINTS
1	9
2	6
3	4
4	3
5	2
6	1

Under this system it was possible for the championship to be won long before the end of the season, robbing the remainder of the season of much of its interest and suspense. To correct this defect the CSI voted, starting with the 1967 season, to divide its championship events into two groups: the first six races and the final five. Now the championship is determined by the five best performances in the first group of races and the four best in the second group. If two or more drivers finish the sea-

4

son with the same number of points the championship is awarded to the driver with the "best-quality" finishing positions, which generally means the driver with most outright victories.

The title of Champion Driver of the World means a great deal. Out of the earth's tens of millions of drivers, there are some thousands who drive racing cars. Of these, twenty — or, at most, thirty — individuals manage to qualify as drivers of Formula One Grand Prix machines. In this group, there are, perhaps, five drivers at any given time whose ability puts them in a class apart from and above the rest. Finally, there is usually one man, perhaps two, who towers above others. Like the great British driver Stirling Moss, he may never win the championship, even though he is a legend in his own time. The greatest talent is forever at the mercy of its luck.

Everything about Grand Prix racing is precarious, including the survival of the sport itself. When it was struggling back to life after the ravages of World War II, Laurence Pomeroy wrote, in his monumental book *The Grand Prix Car:*

Five principal factors have combined in the maintenance of motor racing over the past fifty years. They are the challenge to personal courage, the appeal of pageantry, the desire to use extreme competitive conditions as a forcing ground for technical improvements, the opportunity to advertise by demonstration that the products of one company are superior to all rivals, and last, but by no means least, the means of providing political propaganda to prove the engineering supremacy of one particular nation and the implied supremacy of that nation in all walks of life.

As usual, Pomeroy stated the case with precision and with elegance. His "challenge to personal courage" is the foundation of the sport.

You can't hire a man to become a good, or great, Grand Prix driver; he must be born to the calling. He must have the rarest of endowments, including a fierce appetite for competition and for proving certain things to himself and to others. He has to welcome and seek to pit his skill and courage against the highest of stakes, death. Without this spirit and attitude the sport could not exist.

"The appeal of pageantry," which helps to make Grand Prix racing possible, perhaps can be summed up in one word: spectacle. When it ceases to be thrillingly spectacular — as it did for a good while during the 1.5-liter formula of 1961-1965 — the public begins to look elsewhere for exciting diversion. The sport begins to starve and the formula must be changed in order to lure the public back.

The use of racing as a test laboratory for technical improvements has been a factor in the support of Grand Prix racing, but it never has been essential. The sport would have gone on with or without the active participation of commercial manufacturing firms, which use this facility for the accelerated development of their products under conditions of extreme stress.

Government subsidies of Grand Prix racing have been offered only during periods of crucial international political and economic struggle, and their effectiveness in terms of political propaganda always has been uncertain. In the late 1930's the Italian government granted subsidies for racing to Alfa Romeo, which it also happened to own. But the Alfettas could not compete with the Germans in that period. After the war, and without German competition, the same Alfas were both brilliant and invincible; and the new Italian government and revived industry benefited, by accident, from the Fascist government's investment.

The Nazi government in Germany subsidized Mercedes-Benz and Auto Union to a much greater extent, and the German cars dominated racing in the late '30's. This is *the* one great instance in which such an investment paid off in the fullest measure and in the broadest political and psychological terms. While they were preparing for war the Nazis made capital of this proof of their invincibility in the fields of technology and organization. The investment gave birth to an indelible legend, which postwar Mercedes performances have massively reinforced.

A decisive factor in this equation is Pomeroy's fourth: advertising. This brings us to the core of economic reality in Grand Prix racing today.

Contrary to widespread opinion and in conflict with race-attendance figures, which are almost invariably exaggerated, automobile racing in general and Grand Prix racing in particular have hardly ever paid their own way. Like thoroughbred horse racing, Grand Prix racing has always been a sport of kings, meaning that its existence depends upon massive infusions of outside wealth and not upon its mere box-office draw. Here are some of the costs involved.

To set up a proper Grand Prix circuit costs a minimum of $150,000; to stage a single first-class event costs about the same. Because of the limited number of Grand Prix cars and drivers and because of the tightly packed international racing calendar, only a few top-flight events can be staged on a given circuit in any one season. In the case of Formula One championship races, the limit is one event per year. Race organizers try to balance their profits and losses by staging several diversified events each season, usually two or three, because too many events tend to cheapen the over-all attraction, making what is special seem commonplace.

At present, it is normal for organizers of Grands Prix to pay about $70,000 in starting and prize money in order to assure a field of first-class cars and drivers. Some pay much more.

This heavy expenditure is justified by a variety of facts. Through 1965 the cost of each Grand Prix car averaged around $24,000. With the advent of the 3-liter formula this cost in most cases, leaped to around

7

$38,000. Top-level Grand Prix drivers are now earning between $110,-000 and $140,000 per year. To bring these stars and their costly cars to the starting grid requires money.

The 1966 French Grand Prix, for example, paid about $60,000 in starting money and $20,000 in prize money, or purse; this is standard European practice. It provides good talent and equipment with abundant compensation for its appearance at the starting line, along with good, but not dire, incentive to drive to win. The American system, on the other hand (as at Indianapolis), pays no starting money. The struggle for the purse tends to be a mad and desperate scramble. American oval-track drivers consider the European system to be unsporting, while European drivers consider the American system to be foolhardy and dangerous.

The management of the Watkins Glen circuit has adopted a variation of the two systems for the United States Grand Prix. For its 1966 event it offered $102,400 in prize money, allowing $20,000 for the winner and decreasing amounts for other placements down to $2,800 for the twentieth-place finisher. Since the starting field was limited to twenty entries and transportation costs were paid, there was not a money loser in the race.

These are some of the costs of Grand Prix racing today, and they help to explain why it is anything but self-sufficient. Spectators, even when there are tens of thousands, rarely are numerous enough to enable a given event to break even. How does Grand Prix racing survive? The answer is simple: by the grace of certain oil companies.

Shell has subsidized Ferrari for decades. The last figure I heard, from an authoritative source, was 250 million *lire* per year — $400,000 — which Shell pumps into the Ferrari racing program.

In 1965 Shell-Mex and BP International (based in England) were said to be providing a combined $5.6 to $7.0 million for the support of motor sport, out of which sum a large percentage was earmarked for Grand Prix racing.

In addition to this, numerous Shell and BP national subsidiaries give other important financial support within their own countries. Many other oil companies, such as Esso and Supercortemaggiore, have added more to the coffers. Their motives are not to improve their products through tests in the crucible of speed. Their sole motive is just advertising. It has to be effective advertising in order to go on justifying these astronomical expenditures year after year.

In late 1967 some firms, including BP and Esso, decided that it was not sufficiently effective and withdrew their financial support. This was a grave blow to the sport, but it was almost negligible when compared with the effect of the almost simultaneous withdrawal of Firestone. During its brief "tire war" with Goodyear, both firms had poured millions into subsidiaries for GP racing, but this excessive expense could be tolerated only briefly.

Partly to encourage the continuation of oil-company support, the FIA requires the use of "commercial fuel" in all international formula racing. The implication is that this is "pump fuel" and, indeed, competitors are free to use the pump fuel of the country in which they are racing. The rules also state that any commercial fuel with the highest octane rating that is sold in France, Germany, Great Britain, and Italy may be used or may be replaced by another fuel of similar quality but with a plus tolerance of one octane point. Thus, everyone races on gas that is slightly super-super. It is essentially the fuel that the public buys but undoubtedly it is produced and processed with something more than commercial-grade care.

From the beginning of Grand Prix racing, competing machines have had to conform to certain technical restrictions called formulas. At various times these limitations have restricted vehicle weight, fuel consumption, piston area, or piston displacement. Since World War II piston displacement has been the major factor in each formula, all of which are listed in Appendix A. Appropriately, the premier formula, that for Grand Prix racing on the championship level, is called Formula One.

Builders who create machines for this formula are, with very rare exceptions, small specialists. Even when a big company is involved the machinery is built in a separate racing department, which can and must be isolated from commercial production. Building a racing car is as much an art as a technique, and Grand Prix cars truly are handmade articles. Each builder's case is special.

Great Italian car builder Enzo Ferrari is a man who has made a good living for a good lifetime out of racing. The man has never lived for anything but racing, and he has made it feed him well. With his subsidy from Shell, plus his fat share of the winnings over the years, he prospered as a builder and campaigner exclusively of racing cars. When wealthy friends and fans began asking him to build them one-off road machines around his racing components he stumbled upon a rewarding new sideline. He complains eternally about his hard times but he is hardly to be pitied for them. He is the old fox that all others in the field envy, criticize, and admire. He is the King. When he is gone, Grand Prix racing will not be the same.

Charles and John Cooper — father and son — found their way into Grand Prix racing via tiny one-man racing cars which they began building in 1945. They powered the cars with 500 cc motorcycle engines which they mounted at the rear simply because that was easiest. They were the prophets of the modern Grand Prix car. John has kept his business small but now has an arrangement with British Motors Corporation for the production and marketing of the phenomenal Mini Cooper. Therefore he is not totally dependent on racing luck.

Colin Chapman, of Lotus, has had a similar history. He began with cleverly designed ultra-light roadsters for British scrambles competition — a sort of hill-climbing in the mud. A man of technical and commercial brilliance, he quickly worked his way to the front line of Grand Prix car constructors and campaigners. He followed the Ferrari pattern, first building racing cars and then adding a sideline of road machines built in limited volume. Income from sales of the popular Ford Lotus Cortina has helped Chapman cover his heavy investment in racing.

BRM, British Racing Motors, was established immediately after World War II, with the objective of building a world-beating, all-British Grand Prix car. The car was as complex as it was thrillingly promising, but by the time it was beginning to show its potential the formula was changed and the car was obsolete. Tony Vandervell, a leading manufacturer of engine bearings, bought the BRM assets and made a valiant effort to realize the original goal. He was not able to do so. Vandervell sold the firm and established a new one, starting from scratch. The result was indeed a world-beater — the Vanwall. Then the Owen Organization, a huge and diversified manufacturing complex, picked up BRM for fun and advertising, produced a new series of world-beaters, and to its surprise, soon found its hobby operating at a profit. The credit for this belongs largely to hard-working chief engineer Tony Rudd.

Coventry-Climax (recently absorbed by Jaguar) is an engine-manufacturing firm, which, thanks to the talents of engineer Harry Mundy, produced a portable water pump engine that quickly revealed itself as a magnificent power plant for Grand Prix racing. This led to other designs, which were created specifically for racing. The firm is a commercial supplier to the sport, from which it has, at least temporarily, withdrawn.

Daimler-Benz, manufacturer of Mercedes-Benz cars, is in a similar position. When the huge company goes racing it does so as it would

11

undertake any other publicity campaign. This is not to say that its approach to racing is soulless, since the firm takes the greatest pride in its really glorious racing traditions. But the company goes racing only periodically and only when there seems to be an excellent commercial motive to do so. Alfa Romeo and Lancia share the same coldly practical approach, which is why they have been absent from Grand Prix racing since the 1950's. Those who support racing consistently do so out of passion, and there is supposed to be no room for this emotion in the world of big business.

The only member of the Old Guard of Grand Prix racing who remains a thorough individualist, devoting himself solely to building (and *driving* magnificently!) Grand Prix cars is the shrewd Australian Jack Brabham, three-time Grand Prix champion. But a new wave of builder-driver-individualists is already rising: American Dan Gurney and New Zealander Bruce McLaren are among those who are beginning to shape Grand Prix racing's future.

Meanwhile, the Ford Motor Company appears to be well on its way toward total domination of all forms of major automobile racing. In 1967 it was invincible in Formula Two and almost so in Formula One. In both categories Ford was indebted to the design talents of a young British engineer, Keith Duckworth.

I discussed the subject of Grand Prix racing with top executives of General Motors in the mid-1950's. They had given it considerable thought already and had arrived at the conclusion that there is only one intelligent approach: forget the towering stockpile of talent in the GM Technical Center and sign up the Alfred Neubauers, Rudolf Uhlenhauts, John Coopers, Colin Chapmans, Jack Brabhams, and others who are already wizards of this esoteric art.

Grand Prix racing owes its existence to a small number of mechanics, technicians, engineers, and strategists whose entire vital energy is dedicated to the sport. It also owes its existence to a small but brilliant band of drivers whose dedication has to be even greater, since they put their lives on the line in every race. In the following pages we will meet the greatest of these men and become familiar with the circuits on which they face their moments — their long hours and weeks and years — of truth.

The Grand Prix of Argentina

Autodromo Municipal de la Ciudad de Buenos Aires

There is no country on earth where the passion for automobile racing is more intense than it is in Argentina. Argentine racing began when the first cars were imported — nearly all from the United States — and events for Model-T Fords continue to be an institution there. Races for modified stock cars are innumerable. Auto racing is one of the nation's leading national sports, a fact that helps to explain why this far-from-developed country has produced a number of good-to-great drivers.

Automobile racing became a serious interest of the state when General Juan D. Perón was elected president in 1946. To improve the quality of automotive competition in Argentina, he strongly encouraged the introduction of international Grand Prix racing and helped the Automobile Club of Argentina to obtain a number of GP cars for the use of local drivers. The first Argentine GP was held at Buenos Aires in 1947. For several years the event was won regularly by Italians Gigi Villoresi and Alberto Ascari. Still, from the first, Argentine drivers such as Oscar Galvez and Juan Fangio were among the top three in every race. Buenos Aires is the world's ninth largest city and this new and very thrilling type of racing experience drew really stupendous crowds.

This encouraged Perón to decree, in 1950, the construction of one of the finest road-racing circuits in the world. When it opened on March 9, 1952, the inaugural program stated, "One of the greatest works which General Perón and Eva Perón can point to as a reality of the New Argentina and which reveals their commitment in promoting sport in the country is the 17th of October Autodrome."

Municipal Autodrome, Buenos Aires. View from the well-built pits facing the official tribune and some of the grandstands.

Its name commemorated the date of Perón's accession to power. Many things have changed in Argentina since then, but the Autodrome is finer than ever.

The entire 364-acre complex on the outskirts of Buenos Aires was designed by Argentine government architects and engineers. Nothing about the circuit was imitative of European practice. It was readily conceded by the overseas press that it was incomparable and that spectator facilities "are among the best in the world, vast grandstands having been built to accommodate crowds the size of which defies the imagination of those who have not actually seen them."

"A high technical, architectural and social conception," the Argentines themselves added. Every public convenience was provided: toilets, telephones, bars, restaurants, beautifully landscaped grounds, and practically a city of fine reinforced-concrete grandstands. Parking facilities were almost infinite, with tree-lined access roads almost surrounding the circuit. These roads had their own public-address systems for the efficient direction of traffic. An excellent garage area built of reinforced concrete was provided along with a control tower, press stand, hospital, and pits, all equipped in the most up-to-date manner by the Ministry of Industry and Commerce. It was a source of pride for all of Argentina. It still is.

The original concept was to provide five distinct circuits within the 1.95-mile-periphery track in order to accommodate a variety of types of motor racing. This would seem to have been enough, but the Autodrome's highly diversified and jam-packed year-round racing schedule has made it desirable to add another five, still-different, circuits, for a total of ten.

Circuit Number Two has always been used for Formula One racing, and it is, therefore, known as the International Circuit. It is 2.92 miles long and grandstands extend around almost half its length. It is partly quite fast and partly tortuous. It has three high-speed curves and two 180-degree hairpins. In spite of its huge radius, the large curve that joins the two main straights cannot be taken faster than about 120 MPH since the straights themselves form an angle of about 170 degrees. Traction is excellent and the rate of tire wear constantly is high.

The circuit has a very good safety record. Drivers tend to complain about just one hazard — the heat of the Argentine summer which occurs, of course, in the months of November, December, and January because Argentina is in the Southern Hemisphere. Buenos Aires climate is similar to that of the American Midwest — very humid and often roasting hot. During the 1955 Argentine GP, for example, the unshaded temperature

16

was 140 degrees F. Every car in the race had at least two drivers, some three. There was just one exception: local-boy Fangio. He drove the entire three hours without relief and won. He also was the victor in 1954, 1956, and 1957.

General Perón was deposed in September, 1955, and whatever state aid may have been allotted to the financing of the Grand Prix presumably was withdrawn. It was an extremely expensive event to stage because of the shipping costs of the teams, in addition to starting and prize money. As long as Fangio was on the scene, challenging and beating the world's best, the crowds were like swarms of locusts, and the GP was a practical success. After his retirement in 1959 the race was dropped. A last effort was made in 1960 and then the Argentine Club gave up . . . for the time being.

In 1967, the old spirit was back in full force along with a promising new crop of Argentine drivers, many of whom had been trained by old master Fangio himself. At presstime the Club was negotiating for reinstatement on the championship calendar. The obstacle, as always, was financial; and Argentina was still politically and economically unstable. The local appetite for racing was as strong as ever. At the last Formula Three race of the 1966 season large crowds had to be turned away from "the biggest, most complete, and safest racing course in the world."

The Autodrome is not served by public transport and must be reached by car or taxi. Under normal traffic conditions it is about a half-hour's drive from downtown Buenos Aires, where there are hotel accommodations for everyone.

CIRCUIT LENGTH   2.92 miles, Circuit No. 2
RACE DISTANCE   80 laps—233.60 miles
LAP RECORD   87.43 MPH (race). Moss, 2.5-liter Lotus-Climax

ORGANIZERS	Automóvil Club Argentino, Avenida del Libertador Gral. San Martín 1850, Buenos Aires, Argentina
MONTH	Normally in January

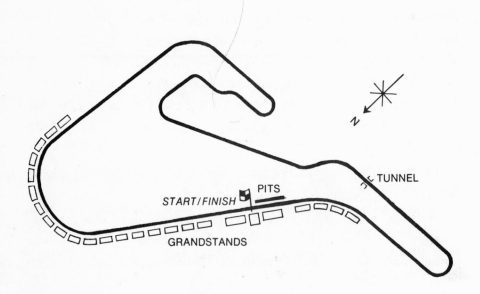

THE GRAND PRIX OF ARGENTINA

YEAR	DRIVER	CAR	WINNING SPEED MPH
1954	Fangio	Maserati	70.2
1955	Fangio	Mercedes-Benz	77.51
1956	Fangio/Musso	Ferrari	79.38
1957	Fangio	Maserati	80.47
1958	Moss	Cooper	83.56
1960	McLaren	Cooper	82.77

The Grand Prix of Belgium

Circuit National de Spa-Francorchamps

This road circuit was, until 1966, the fastest in the world. It started in 1921 as the scene of a mild, 375-mile sports-car race. In 1925 the GP of Europe was held there and was won by Antonio Ascari's P2 Alfa Romeo at 74.56 MPH. The first Belgian GP took place there in 1930; the winning team of "Williams" and Caberto Conelli drove a Bugatti for ten hours at an average of 82.01 MPH. The highest winning speed in the prewar period was Rudi Hasse's 104.70 in a 5.5-liter Auto Union. In 1950, Juan Fangio won at 109.98 and ten years later Brabham set the still-fastest average for the GP at 133.62 MPH.

While some race organizers and circuit managements give at least lip service to slowing down the sport, those behind the Belgian GP have gone all-out to make possible ever-higher speeds. Sharp, slow corners have been eliminated so that only one remains, at La Source, and all the curves are great, sweeping, high-speed ones. As it stands now, this very long circuit is as tricky, dangerous, and unforgiving as it is fast. It frightens brave men who know that their slightest error — or the next man's — can send them hurtling to probable destruction.

Surprisingly enough, in view of its high speed, this circuit's "straights" are not straight; they are slightly winding. Spa's close to nine-mile series of high-speed curves calls for driving on the razor's edge and sorts out talent as few other circuits can.

Surprisingly, too, in view of its speed, the circuit is not on level ground. Instead, it rushes across the floor of a wide valley, mounts and traverses a mountain flank to the head of the valley, then returns along

Spa-Francorchamps. The circuit's one slow turn is La Source Hairpin.

the opposite flank, and finally descends to the starting point on the valley floor. Thus, over a large portion of the course, running off the pavement means colliding with a mountainside or dropping off it.

Spa's setting is at least as beautiful as that of the Nürburgring or Clermont-Ferrand. It is set in the gentle pine-clad mountains of the Ardennes Forest, about 30 miles south of Liége and 10 miles from the German border. The valley floor lies at an elevation of about 1,150 feet and is the greenest of pasture land, studded with an occasional picturesque village; the surrounding slopes rise another 900 feet. It is a won-

20

derful circuit for the spectator, with its panoramic views from the main grandstand and other vantage points.

The town of Spa is about 6 miles away from the start-finish line near the small village of Francorchamps. Spa was a flourishing health resort before World War I and still maintains a great many of the prewar hotels. Another relic is its gambling casino, now patronized mainly by German tourists and sometimes called "the Ardennes' Revenge."

Only two or three races per year are held on the circuit: the Grand Prix, the 24 Hours of Spa-Francorchamps, and it is included occasionally as one of the "circuit legs" of the *Tour de France*.

In order to conduct any of these events the organizers must endure enormous difficulties. The basic problem is that the circuit is laid out over public thoroughfares and local villagers do not enjoy having their roads blocked. Moreover, they do not appreciate invasions of up to

Spa-Francorchamps. The start-finish line and pit area.

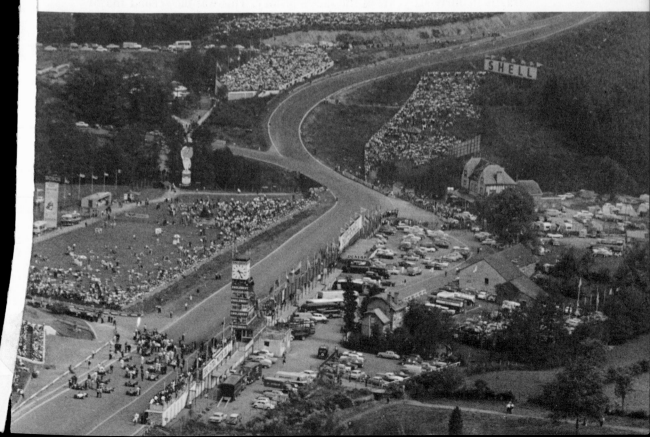

40,000 spectators and herds of roaring machines, which unnerve the livestock, their modest local wealth. Nor do they relish the greatly increased forest-fire hazard.

Each time a race is to be held, organizers must go to each of the tiny communities that will be affected and wring contracts from each of the responsible authorities. It is doing things the hard way.

Everyone regards Spa-Francorchamps with mixed feelings. Another of its disadvantages is that its roadbeds are old and battered in many spots. The resulting rough surface is very hard on suspension systems, which often fail, and adds to the over-all danger. Still, Spa is unique in many ways. There is no handy alternative, and the practice of holding the Belgian GP there is not likely to be abandoned in the foreseeable future.

It is one of the most heroic and "hairy" of the championship combats. The 1966 race was the most dramatic, and came close to being the most tragic, in thirty-six years of the race's history. This was the second major race of the 3-liter formula and practice times on the Friday preceding the race promised the devastation of all existing records.

On Sunday afternoon fifteen cars took the starting flag under blackening skies. The howling pack was barely a third of the way around the course when "It's raining at Malmedy" was blandly announced over the PA. The drivers had no way of knowing of this, and they hit the downpour and streaming pavement without warning, doing about 130 MPH and already committed to the next turn. Jo Bonnier hit Mike Spence; Denis Hulme hit Jo Siffert; Bob Bondurant flew off the road, hit a tree, and went end-over-end; Jochen Rindt and Richie Ginther sat helplessly, their cars spinning like tops; Jack Brabham missed ramming a house by inches; Graham Hill spun, stopped, and watched Jackie Stewart's BRM crash down a gully. Hill and Bondurant leaped from their cars and

22

rushed to free Stewart, who was trapped in wreckage that might burst into flame at any moment.

This was the extent of the drama. By a miracle no one was killed, nor were there any grave injuries. That race at Francorchamps, which turned into a dull procession of five cars, should have driven home to the racing world the need for a rain-warning system on long courses where such surprises can occur. The 1967 race was a GP landmark for the United States, thanks to Dan Gurney's Eagle win at record speed.

Many of the faithful who flock to Spa-Francorchamps stay in Brussels and make the approximate two-and-a-half hour trip by car. Many others stay in Spa's numerous second-rate hotels. A few find accommodations in villages at and near the circuit. Camping and trailer space scarcely exist; in all of crowded little Belgium there is room for only about 3,000 campers.

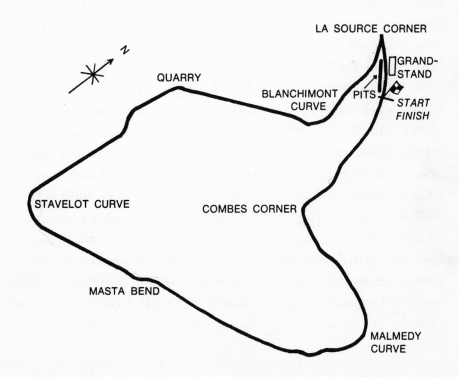

CIRCUIT LENGTH	8.75 miles
RACE DISTANCE	28 laps–245 miles
LAP RECORD	149.8 MPH (race). Surtees, Honda, 1968
ORGANIZERS	Circuit de Spa-Francorchamps, 21, av. des Cerisiers, Brussels, Belgium
MONTH	Normally in June

THE GRAND PRIX OF BELGIUM
(Spa-Francorchamps Circuit)

YEAR	DRIVER	CAR	WINNING SPEED MPH
1950	Fangio	Alfa Romeo	109.98
1951	Farina	Alfa Romeo	114.26
1952	Ascari	Ferrari	103.13–F2
1953	Ascari	Ferrari	112.47–F2
1954	Fangio	Maserati	115.08
1955	Fangio	Mercedes-Benz	118.83
1956	Collins	Ferrari	118.44
1958	Brooks	Vanwall	129.92
1960	Brabham	Cooper	133.62
1961	P. Hill	Ferrari	128.15
1962	Clark	Lotus	131.89
1963	Clark	Lotus	114.10
1964	Clark	Lotus	132.79
1965	Clark	Lotus	117.16
1966	Surtees	Ferrari	113.93
1967	Gurney	Eagle-Weslake	145.9
1968	McLaren	Matra-Ford	147.13

24

The British Grand Prix

Silverstone

The first British Grand Prix (then called the "English") was held by the Royal Automobile Club (RAC) on the historic Brooklands Track in 1926. There was a second installment in 1927 and then an absence of big-time road racing from "The Sceptered Isle" until the years 1935 through 1938 when the Axis-grinding Alfas, Mercedes-Benz, and Auto Unions took part in and, of course, dominated the Donnington Park Grand Prix, an unofficial substitute for the "British."

The war was no sooner over than a mounting groundswell of motor-racing passion began breaking out all over England, and people began racing anything and everything, anywhere. "Anywhere" included un-used and slightly used air strips and air bases. One of the latter was Silverstone, about midway between London and Birmingham. There, in 1948, the RAC organized the third official British GP. It attracted a fine international starting field and the 250-mile race was won by Gigi Villoresi in a Maserati.

This historic event, staged with the assistance of the British Racing Drivers' Club (BRDC), astonished everyone by the immense crowds it attracted. Something big obviously had been let loose. The RAC, content with having gotten GP racing in England off to a promising start, invited the BRDC to run the event in the future.

As we have seen, staging a major racing event is an extremely costly business. Since the BRDC's coffers were hardly overflowing, the club's secretary, Desmond Scannell, decided to look for an angel and had the inspiration to call on the managements of London's major newspapers. This quest brought him, early in 1949, to Tom Blackburn, now chairman

Silverstone. It is the most famous of the world's airport circuits. This 1963 view shows Jo Bonnier leading Richie Ginther. Both are driving BRM's.

of the Beaverbrook Newspaper Company and then a top executive of that chain's *London Daily Express*.

Blackburn was acutely sensitive to the automotive mania sweeping his country and much of the world; and he was attentive to Scannell's every word. Blackburn's job was to sell newspapers, not to make direct profits out of racing. But he correctly reasoned that if a great daily could be intimately associated in the public mind with a sporting event that gripped the interest of millions, then the effect on the paper's circulation could be quite bracing. The BRDC secretary asked for financial help until the club could afford to stage major events at Silverstone. He estimated that this would take at least five years. Blackburn shook his hand saying, "If it takes ten we'll still stand behind you." It took exactly ten years, but the relationship was so mutually satisfactory that it stands to this day.

One thing upon which Blackburn insisted was that everything — cars, drivers, spectacle, and spectator facilities — all be second to none, which was merely giving voice to the BRDC's own fondest dreams. Thus with the paper's editorial and financial backing, the 1949 race, with its stellar field and lavish promotion, was the most successful motor race ever held in Britain up to that time. About 100,000 spectators were on hand for the unprecedented show, and they have been coming in similar numbers ever since.

In 1950, what had been called the BRDC *Daily Express* International Trophy Race was assigned the title of British GP and, for that year, the Grand Prix of Europe — a perfectly meaningless title and honor that the FIA confers upon a different championship event each year. Along with this, the British GP was recognized as one of the Grandes Epreuves counting toward the just-created drivers' championship. The event was graced by the presence of King George VI, Queen Elizabeth, and the Princesses. The race was dominated by the invincible Alfa Romeo Al-

27

fettas, in one of which a newcomer named Fangio made one of his first important European appearances. This race was such a success that other newspapers began scrambling to back races on other circuits and a new era was born in the economics and in the very life of the sport.

It would be difficult to find very many admirers of airport circuits as such. They are inherently flat and featureless; and as a rule they are as boring to drivers as they are to spectators.

But Silverstone, bleak though it may be, has its host of supporters. It is, after all, Britain's fastest circuit. Its main grandstand offers spectators an action-packed view of the cars barreling out of fast Woodcote Corner. In contrast, the main stands at the Monza and Nürburgring courses, for example, are in the middle of long, relatively dull straights. Then there is the mighty role that Silverstone has played in the development of the car and driver superiority Britain enjoys today.

The concrete of the main perimeter circuit was resurfaced with asphalt in the early 1950's; it is quite smooth and causes only average tire wear in spite of the high speeds permitted by the predominance of straightaways. Most of the eight curves are broad, sweeping, and very fast. The slowest and trickiest is Becket's Corner and the fastest is Chapel Curve, just beyond it; they are wonderful to watch. Midway between these two bends the spectator can contemplate the ruins of the Chapel of St. Thomas à Becket, the celebrated Archbishop of Canterbury who was murdered on the steps of Canterbury Cathedral in 1170.

Silverstone's pits are located opposite the main grandstand. There is no permanent garage area and the teams work out of their vans, which is standard practice in Britain. Many of the GP drivers own and fly their own light aircraft and land at the circuit. The weather, of course, is typically English, usually threatening to rain and often doing so.

The British Grand Prix

CIRCUIT LENGTH	2.937 miles
RACE DISTANCE	80 laps–240 miles
LAP RECORD	121.20 MPH (race). Hulme, Brabham-Repco, 1967
ORGANIZERS	British Racing Drivers' Club, Ltd., 9 Down St., London, W1, England
MONTH	Normally in July

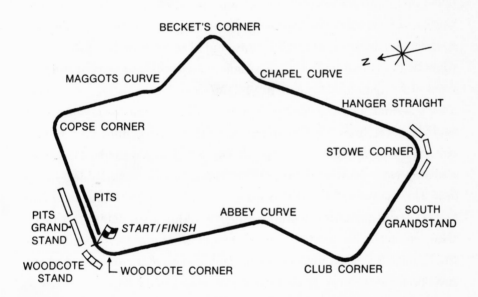

Aintree

The Aintree Grand National steeplechase circuit has been sacred ground to the horse-racing world since 1839. Its location, five miles northeast of the somewhat grim industrial seaport city of Liverpool, may do nothing for its glamor but its proximity to such great Midlands population centers as Coventry, Manchester, Birmingham, and the Beatles' own home town, plus an exceptional network of convenient access roads and highways, all help Aintree in drawing some of the world's most colossal racing crowds.

The overnight success of Silverstone was duly noted by the Grand National's equestrian management, which lost little time in forming the Aintree Automobile Racing Company, Ltd. The body then voted to wrap a three-mile asphalt road course around the steeplechase course, adding a looping excursion through its infield. In this way all of the horse track's permanent facilities were made to serve the ends of motor racing too. These facilities include spacious parking areas, numerous restaurants, and magnificent, ornate nineteenth-century grandstands. They have a seating capacity of 20,000 and — what is really remarkable — they provide a view of almost the entire circuit. In addition to this there is a natural grandstand in the form of a high banking about 2,000 feet long; it runs the full length of Sefton Straight and all of the course can be seen from its summit. The total spectator facilities have a capacity of about 200,000 persons, meaning that Aintree can accommodate almost as many people as Nürburgring within a tiny fraction of the German circuit's huge area.

The dead-flat, almost treeless circuit is blanketed with well-kept grass and, depending upon the wind, the odors from nearby factory chimneys. The grandstands are situated at the exit of the very interesting Tatt's Corner and at the start of the 3,000 foot main straight. Of the circuit's eight corners only two are reasonably fast, the remainder being of 90

Aintree is set in highly industrial surroundings. Here Stirling Moss (Vanwall) leads the 1957 Grand Prix of Europe.

degrees or less and, therefore, not popular with many drivers. Except for the fast esses near Tatt's Corner all curves are joined by dead-straight pavement, which makes driving at Aintree a succession of drag races interspersed with a great deal of braking, downshifting, and very hard cornering. The circuit may be highly artificial as a road course but it does give spectators a lot to watch and drivers a lot to do. It is excellent from all standpoints of safety.

The first automobile race took place here in May, 1954, and the first Grand Prix in July of the following year. This was shortly after the Le Mans disaster; and since the Grands Prix of France, Germany, and Switzerland had been canceled, Aintree's importance loomed unexpectedly in the championship calendar, which had shrunk to just six

Aintree. This is just a small fraction of this circuit's immense spectator capacity.

events. The race was one of Mercedes-Benz's greatest victories as the four cars Mercedes entered filled the first four finishing positions. They were driven by Stirling Moss, Juan Fangio, Karl Kling, and Piero Taruffi, Moss pegging the lap record at 89.70 MPH. Perfect weather had helped to draw a crowd of 150,000, which cheered itself hoarse as Moss became the first Briton to win a British GP. He repeated his Aintree victory two years later at the wheel of a Vanwall, well in front of the Ferrari team.

Following the 1955 race the RAC adopted the practice of awarding the British GP to Silverstone and Aintree on alternate years until 1962, when the event took place at Aintree for the second year running. This was done in recognition of the fiftieth anniversary of the British Automobile Racing Club (BARC), the official organizer of the British Grand Prix at Aintree. The BARC enjoys the reputation of staging racing contests that are ideally managed without a trace of the ponderous officialdom that burdens most similar events on the Continent.

The British Grand Prix

Whatever drivers' feelings may be, races at Aintree are a spectators' delight. The circuit is reached conveniently by electric train from nearby Liverpool, where hotel accommodations abound.

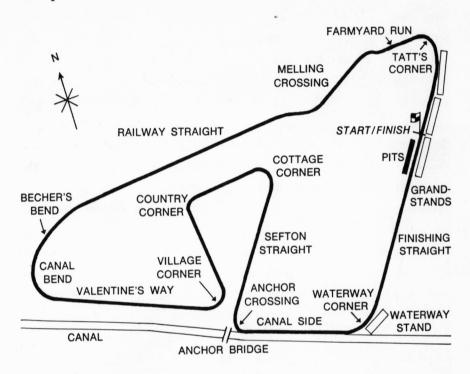

CIRCUIT LENGTH	3.0 miles
RACE DISTANCE	75 laps—225 miles
LAP RECORD	93.91 MPH (race). Clark, 1.5-liter Lotus 25, 1962
ORGANIZERS	Aintree Automobile Racing Co., Ltd., Racecourse Offices, Aintree, Liverpool 9, England British Automobile Racing Club, 5-6 Argyll Street, London, W.1, England
:ONTH	Normally in July

33

Brands Hatch

Brands Hatch is the newest of the British GP circuits; it also is the oldest.

One day in 1926 a group of bicyclists, bound homeward after a 150-mile outing, came upon an expanse of undulating meadowland on the main road (now A20) from London to Maidstone. It had the form of a natural amphitheater and, being right-thinking young men, the cyclists recognized it as an ideal potential race course. They wheeled down to the cottage — which, of course, was called Brands Hatch — and persuaded the farmer that, in addition to cultivating mushrooms, he could cultivate a few shillings each weekend by letting them hold races there. He agreed, and added to his income by selling refreshments to his new visitors. In 1928 the motorcycle fraternity joined the bicyclists in the enjoyment of this outstanding grass track.

Racing was lovely at Brands until the war, when the British Army took the little track over for its own purposes. It won the flattery of becoming a military objective and was often bombed by the Germans. But as soon as the war was over and fuel was available again, motorcyclists were back in action. They rerouted the track around bomb craters, and by 1947 Brands was the finest and best-known motorcycle grass track in Britain. It flourished so that it had to have a director, and Joe Francis found $30,000 with which to pay for the paving of the one-mile, kidney-shaped circuit with asphalt.

This was the period when 500 cc Formula Three racing was being introduced, with infinite credit due to John Cooper and his father, Charles. These rear-engined *monoposti* — true forerunners of modern GP machines — used motorcycle engines for power and, what is rare, this was a period of intimacy between people who raced on two wheels and those who raced on four. The bike crowd told the 500 crowd about Brands and it was Ken Gregory, a pioneer of the 500 cc Club and, later, Stirling Moss's manager, who set up the first automobile race there —

Brands Hatch. Many structures have been added since this aerial photo was made in 1960. Note the almost all-inclusive view from the grandstand.

for 500's, of course. That first race took place on April 16, 1950, and drew 10,000 spectators. "But," said John Cooper recently, "it was just a homely club affair; like a big garden party compared with what followed." Part of what followed was Brands's emergence as "the greatest racing-driver nursery in the world." One of its "babies" was Stirling Moss.

On the heels of Brands's emergence as an automotive circuit, a nearby horse-racing track was sold to housing developers. Representatives of Brands and of the 500 cc Club rushed in and bought the steel grandstand for a song. They dismantled it, moved it to Brands, bolted it together again, and made theirs the first automotive circuit in Britain to have a

35

Brands Hatch. A trackside view during the 1964 British Grand Prix.

permanent grandstand. This was the beginning of a policy of constant improvement. It led, in the winter of 1959–1960, to the enlargement of the circuit to 2.65 miles and, in 1964, to the holding of the first British GP at Brands Hatch.

The course is quite undulating. The first turn, Paddock Hill Bend, is the most tricky of the eleven. It is partially blind, has a negative camber, and a pronounced hump; its limit is about 90 MPH.

The third corner, Druid's Hill Bend, is the tightest on the course; it is a large hairpin around which few drivers can top 45 MPH. There is a severe dip under Pilgrim's Overpass, where sparks fly as cars bottom in passing it. The entire circuit is exciting, both for drivers and spectators,

36

and the photographic opportunities are excellent. Graham Hill says, "There's not a single orthodox corner in the whole collection. They either drop away or climb or else have some other odd feature." In all, there are three marked dips on the course and at least two corners that are blind before the apex, meaning that drivers must set their steering for a curve they cannot see. Brands is a real road-racing course and anyone in England who mentions it in the same breath with Silverstone is begging for a fight.

In the process of winning the first Brands GP in 1964, Jim Clark set a lap record of precisely 100.0 MPH in his 1.5-liter Lotus-Climax. During the 1966 race it was expected that the 3-liter cars would make mincemeat of this figure. But only two could improve upon it — Jack Brabham and his teammate, Denis Hulme. They finished the race first and second.

37

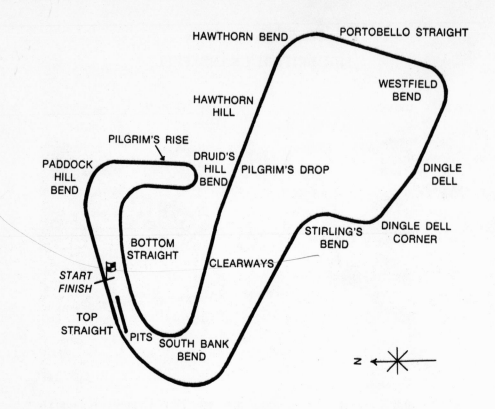

CIRCUIT LENGTH	2.65 miles
RACE DISTANCE	80 laps—212 miles
LAP RECORD	106.53 MPH (race). Clark, Lotus-Ford, 1967
ORGANIZERS	Brands Hatch Circuit, Ltd., Fawkham, near Dartford, Kent, England
MONTH	Normally in July

THE BRITISH GRAND PRIX

YEAR	DRIVER	CAR	WINNING SPEED MPH	CIRCUIT
1950	Farina	Alfa Romeo	90.95	Silverstone
1951	Gonzales	Ferrari	96.11	Silverstone
1952	Ascari	Ferrari	90.92	Silverstone F2
1953	Ascari	Ferrari	92.97	Silverstone F2
1954	Gonzales	Ferrari	89.69	Silverstone
1955	Moss	Mercedes-Benz	86.47	Aintree
1956	Fangio	Ferrari	98.65	Silverstone
1957	Brooks/Moss	Vanwall	86.80	Aintree
1958	Collins	Ferrari	102.05	Silverstone
1959	Brabham	Cooper	89.88	Aintree
1960	Brabham	Cooper	108.69	Silverstone
1961	von Trips	Ferrari	83.91	Aintree
1962	Clark	Lotus	92.25	Aintree
1963	Clark	Lotus	107.75	Silverstone
1964	Clark	Lotus	94.14	Brands Hatch
1965	Clark	Lotus	112.02	Silverstone
1966	Brabham	Brabham-Repco	95.48	Brands Hatch
1967	Clark	Lotus-Ford	117.64	Silverstone
1967	Brabham	Brabham-Repco	82.72	Brands Hatch
1968	Siffert	Lotus-Ford	104.83	Brands Hatch

The Grand Prix of Canada

Until 1960 sports-car racing in Canada took place exclusively on airport circuits, with all their limitations and drawbacks. Then the sport there began to come of age. The Westwood Circuit near New Westminster in British Columbia was built, and the groundbreaking began on Mosport Park, about 50 miles from Toronto, in eastern Canada and within easy traveling distance of the vast population centers that lie just south of the border. Mosport's first race, the Players 200, was held on June 25, 1961, starting an uninterrupted march from success to success. Mosport's participation in the Can-Am — the Canadian American Challenge Cup — annual series of top-level sports car races brought the track international fame and prestige. Then, in 1967, for the first time in Canada, Mosport staged an event for Indianapolis-type cars. But the high point of Canadian racing history to date was Canada's first Formula One Championship Grand Prix, held on August 17, 1967.

Mosport was created by the British Empire Motor Club of Canada, whose members conceived the idea and pooled $30,000 for the purchase of 500 acres of fine, rolling country studded with woods and streams. This outlay, of course, was only the beginning and later another $250,000 was needed to convert the raw terrain into an outstanding racing circuit. The Club had its share of good salesmen, and they persuaded a dozen Canadian firms in the beverage, tobacco, and automotive industries to subscribe this substantial amount.

The Mosport track is laid out over almost 2.5 miles of asphalt pavement that twists and dives through nine tight turns and one sweeping curve; it has a 4000-foot straightaway. Several of its corners involve blind

Mosport. Site of the first Canadian GP in 1967, Mosport Park provides maximum spectator freedom, beautiful scenery, and a thorough test of men and machines.

rises with zero visibility ahead and two of its crests are followed by sudden, steep downhill descents. It is an arduous test for drivers, but its safety record has been good. Stirling Moss, who won the first Players 200 there, pronounced Mosport one of the three outstanding road circuits in the world.

Spectators agree. The pastoral setting is beautiful and the undulating terrain is dotted with commanding vantage points and natural grandstands. Spectators are free to circulate around the entire circuit, either by interior roads or by roads outside of the park itself. The cost of admission provides unlimited entry and exit through the several service gates.

41

Mosport is about an hour's drive from metropolitan Toronto, where lodging accommodations are plentiful. And there are many good, comfortable motels and hotels near the circuit and the town of Bowmanville, Ontario, 8 miles away. Good highways link the region with Detroit and Buffalo.

The first Grand Prix of Canada, held in 1967, brought seventeen starters to the line, including all major luminaries with the exception of John Surtees/Honda. Practice on the preceding days took place in fine weather and Jim Clark, the favorite, drove his Lotus-Ford to a new lap record of 1M 22.4s.

Rain had been predicted for race day and the skies were overcast but no rain fell until ten minutes before the start, when a steady drizzle began. This was the first rain of the entire Formula One season and it began too close to the start of the race to permit the teams' changing to wet weather tires. No one wanted to risk the change to faster-wearing rain tires beforehand.

Clark took full advantage of his pole position, setting up a cautious lead on the greasy surface. Within four laps Denis Hulme had overtaken him, and the race became a seesaw duel between these leaders. The rain let up, the track dried, fast racing began and Clark turned two laps in a row at a consistent 1M 23.9s. Then the rain began anew. Clark dropped out with a drenched electrical system and Hulme was forced to make two emergency pit stops in quick succession. Hulme's boss, Jack Brabham, took over the lead, which he held serenely until the 90th and last lap, making this the third one-two victory of the season for Brabham-Repco cars, as Hulme still managed to finish in second place. Dan Gurney finished third in an Eagle, one lap behind the leaders.

The race proved that racing enthusiasm in Canada is unsquelchable and has a glorious future. In spite of the forecast of rain and its ample fulfilment, 55,000 fearless fans were on hand to see racing history made.

That number was only one thousand less than Canada's all-time record, which also, of course, belongs to Mosport. And so does the record for one of the slowest races in modern Grand Prix history.

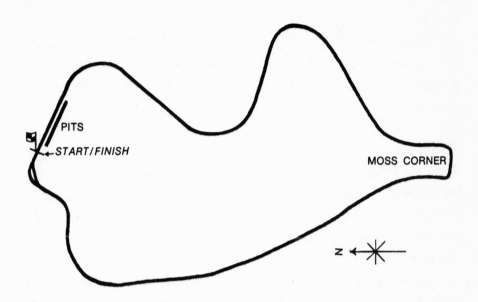

CIRCUIT LENGTH   2.459 miles

RACE DISTANCE   90 laps–220 miles

LAP RECORD   106.4 MPH (race). Clark, Lotus-Ford, 1967

ORGANIZERS   Canadian Racing Drivers Assn., Toronto

MONTH   Normally in August

THE GRAND PRIX OF CANADA

YEAR	DRIVER	CAR	WINNING SPEED MPH	CIRCUIT
1967	Brabham	Brabham-Repco	82.72	Mosport

The French Grand Prix

Grand Prix of the Automobile Club of France

The French Grand Prix — the GP of the ACF — is the very first to be established and claims to date back to 1895. It is not to be confused with the Grand Prix of France, which was launched by the *Automobile Club de La Sarthe* at Le Mans in 1911. The GP of the ACF is the original Grande Epreuve.

Reims

Until the 1966 French GP, Reims enjoyed the reputation of being the second fastest road circuit in the world. Then Surtees lapped there at 144.6 MPH, Brabham won the 247-mile race at an average of almost 137 MPH, and Reims became Number One for sheer speed. Another of Raymond "Toto" Roche's ambitions was fulfilled.

In most reports on racing at Reims you will find some mention of Toto Roche. Usually it's criticism ranging from bitter to savage. He usually reserves for himself the right to flag the start and finish of every major event there, and while his theatrics may please the grandstand crowds they give the drivers fits. With some reason. For example, the start he gave the GP in 1960 was so unorthodox that there were multiple pile-ups on the line and several good machines and drivers were eliminated from the race. As Graham Hill has said, Roche "raises the flag whenever he feels like it after the half-minute signal [it was *before* in 1960]. He then drops it and runs for his life. He has to do this because he is usually standing in the middle of the track. One of these days, I fear, somebody will get him." This is the extent of what most people, including the drivers, know about Roche. This and that he obviously is *un original*, as they say in French — a character.

44

*Reims. The main straight during the 1961 French GP. The Ferraris of **Phil Hill**, Count von Trips, and Richie Ginther lead, left to right.*

He is that. Short, fat, witty, truculent, domineering, and a mono-maniac. His circuit is everything to him. When his track was only 10 meters wide he filibustered and lobbied and railroaded a regulation into the International Sporting Code that limited *all* GP circuits to that width. When the government widened his own roads he ignored all his old arguments and began a new (and, of course, successful) battle to have the maximum width increased. He is a tyrant and a terror, but with a wonderful, saving sense of humor. What few people know is that Reims is Roche's single-handed creation. When he is no longer there, one of the world's finest racing plants will remain. What will become of it without his driving force remains to be seen.

It was the announcement of the beginning of work on the Montlhéry Autodrome near Paris that planted the idea in young Roche's mind, the idea of creating the world's finest road-racing course in the flat country-side of his own part of France, Champagne. "Folly — it will never amount to anything," everyone said. But Roche started out by remaking (to use his own word) the proud old Automobile Club of Champagne. He bulldozed away every obstacle in his path. Thirty-five years later he appraised his life's work in the words, "The Reims Circuit is there. That's all."

Aside from the inherently monotonous, ultra-high-speed nature of the track itself, Reims stands as the model that designers of other fine, permanent circuits would like to be able to imitate. It is more than a circuit; it is a monument, a showplace.

Name the facilities for the needs or convenience of public, press, or contestants, and they're there, in abundance. Instead of a pages-long list let one example typify the rest: the garage area, with its large reinforced concrete buildings, can accommodate more than 5,000 vehicles.

While Roche has fretted over the rustic decor of his many restaurants and looked after the herd of native sheep that keep his vast, grassy acre-

Reims. This exciting hill on the otherwise generally level course is called La Garenne.

age neatly mowed, the track itself has been eternally on his mind. He is an expert on paving materials and methods, and he is given universal credit for having a superior track. The smoothness of the surface was achieved through the use of Barber Greene paving machinery from the United States of America. The outstanding adhesion it offers, even when very wet, is a result of much research. The asphalt mixture used absorbs considerable oil and gasoline without becoming slippery. There is an escape route for every corner and the entire track is bordered by a very low, outward-tilting curb, which is painted white.

Unlike the directors of many circuits Roche attends most of the European Grands Prix. He is always looking for good new ideas to take home to Reims.

The original course, called the Permanent Road Circuit, was inaugurated in 1925 and the Grand Prix of the Marne (for sports cars) was held there from that time until 1937. In 1938, 1939, and 1948 it was selected for the French GP, and in 1950 Reims was awarded Grande Epreuve status.

This 4.44-mile course was used for GP racing through 1951. In 1952 work began on the addition of another .72 miles of public highways and in 1953 the 5.16-mile Competition Road Circuit was complete. Then Roche went to work streamlining it, rounding off hairpins and straightening and banking curves. Grades of up to 4.5 percent add to its interest.

The course was in its present fast form in 1960 when Brabham, in a 2.5-liter Cooper-Climax, reduced the lap record to 2M 17.5s or 135.40 MPH. This time never was threatened during the 1.5-liter formula, the record being Clark's 2M 21.6s in 1962. During the French GP of 1966 — the third championship race of the 3-liter formula — records tumbled, and Reims won the distinction of being the fastest road course in the world.

Reims in the summer tends to be extremely hot and humid and its police, like those of Monza and Zandvoort, irritable. Lodging usually is not a problem in the beautiful cathedral city of Reims, just five miles away, and there are good camping facilities nearby. The famous international 12 Hours of Reims sports-car race is a thrilling curtain-raiser for the GP and begins at midnight before the big Formula One event.

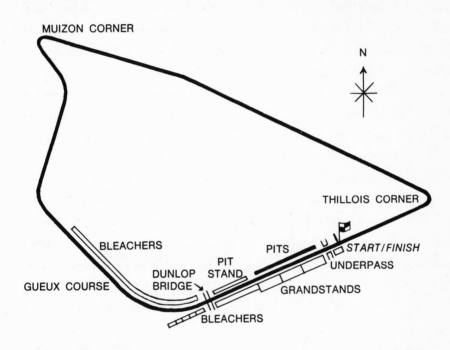

CIRCUIT LENGTH	5.16 miles
RACE DISTANCE	48 laps–247.68 miles
LAP RECORD	142.09 MPH (race). Bandini, 3-liter Ferrari, 1966
ORGANIZERS	Association Sportive de l'Automobile Club de Champagne, 3 Blvd. de la Paix, 51 Reims, France
MONTH	Normally in late June

Rouen

Rouen is a beautiful industrial city about 80 miles northwest of Paris. Near there in 1950 the Sports Association of the Automobile Club of Normandy created the circuit of Rouen-les-Essarts in the gently rolling Rouvray Forest. The original circuit was 3.16 miles around and consisted of a stretch of National Route 840, a section of secondary road and a patched-up logging trail. This was quite good enough for the sports-car and Formula Three races for which it was intended, but in 1951 improvements were made to the surface and a Formula Two race was held there. This was successful enough to resound throughout the French racing world and in 1952 — only its third year — Rouen was chosen for the GP of the ACF. It too was a Formula Two event that year.

The popularity of the picturesque and challenging circuit continued to grow, and its yearly racing calendar became steadily more full. The organizers kept plowing profits back into the improvement of the plant and in 1955, with government approval, they laid another 0.9 miles of pavement. Good grandstands, restaurants, and other permanent structures were added to the 4.06-mile circuit, and in 1957 it was awarded its first Formula One championship race. This GP of the ACF was won by Juan Fangio in a Maserati with Luigi Musso, Lancia-Ferrari, setting the fastest lap at 2M 22.4s — 102.77 MPH.

The next French GP to be held at Rouen was in 1962, with terrible Toto Roche as official starter. This time Dan Gurney gave Porsche its first and only Formula One championship victory, and Graham Hill, BRM, reduced the lap record to 2M 16.9s — 106.90 MPH.

The seventieth anniversary of the world's first road race — Paris to Rouen — fell in 1964. To commemorate the occasion the ACF, which was celebrating *its* fiftieth anniversary, brought the French GP back to Rouen. The organizers resurfaced the track in honor of the occasion and again Gurney won brilliantly, this time in a Brabham-Climax. Jack

50

Rouen. The famous Nouveau Monde Hairpin and its natural amphitheater.

Brabham in a similar car chopped the lap record during the race to 2M 11.4s — 111.37 MPH. It was a historic day for Brabham, since Gurney's was the first championship victory for a Brabham car.

After the race Gurney was asked what he would drive to win the next Rouen Formula One GP, to be held in 1968. "Oh," he laughed, "I'll try to make it an American car." They thought, at the time, that he was kidding. Just over two years later his All American Racers Eagle made its debut at Monza.

The Rouen circuit runs through densely wooded hill country, and it

51

climbs and dips over a range of 450 feet. For all concerned it is far more interesting than Reims' great full-throttle triangle. It is a medium-fast course, slower than Silverstone but faster than Zandvoort.

From the starting line the cars boom over a blind rise, then shoot steeply downhill through a roller-coaster series of fast left-and-right bends to the hairpin at Nouveau Monde, which is taken at about 25 MPH. Then the road climbs an almost 7 percent grade to the very steep Sanson Curve, which is taken in second gear at about 50 MPH. The course levels out, makes a 145 MPH right, then a short straight to the semi-hairpin called the Scierie Curve. At this point the smooth asphalt gives way to paving stones and just beyond this bend is a stretch of rough concrete, all of which gives suspension systems a good pounding. The asphalt resumes and leads through a 115 MPH right onto the main straight, on which better than 145 MPH can be reached. At this speed the cars shoot over the blind hump again, the drivers hoping the road beyond will be clear. Two cars were wrecked in 1964 because it was not.

Rouen has this shortcoming in the matter of driver safety, plus some nasty drainage ditches and, in common with most hilly circuits, it puts a special premium on not going off the road; there are some severe drops.

From the spectators' standpoint Rouen is excellent for watching even if it is difficult to see large portions of the course from most vantage points. For spectator safety it is very good. The hilly slopes themselves serve as fine, well-protected, natural grandstands.

In common with nearly all GP organizers today, those of Rouen stage a whole festival of speed in connection with their Grands Prix. A specialty here is the Cup of the Golden Age: a 12-lap contest for historic racing cars built between the two World Wars. The circuit can accommodate about 50,000 spectators and the nearby city is prepared to house them. There is a large and attractive camping area behind the start-finish-line grandstand.

Rouen. The Nouveau Monde Hairpin is in the distance. The view is truly park-like.

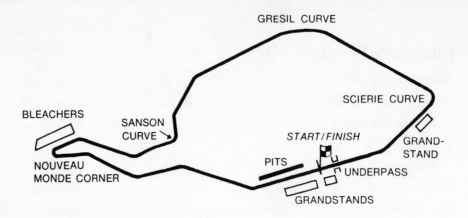

CIRCUIT LENGTH	4.06 miles
RACE DISTANCE	57 laps–231.7 miles, 1964
LAP RECORD	111.37 MPH (race). Brabham, Brabham-Climax, 1964
ORGANIZERS	Association Sportive de l'Automobile Club Normand, 46, rue Général-Giraud, 76 Rouen, France
MONTH	Normally in June/July

54

Clermont–Ferrand

As mentioned earlier, the whole tradition of international Grand Prix racing began with the Gordon Bennett Cup Races, which were organized in France between 1900 and 1905 and which were replaced the following year by the Grand Prix of the ACF.

The organization of the 1905 race fell to the ACF, as it had before, and the French club solicited propositions from communities that would like to host the great event. Many proposals were received but only two towns offered to share in footing the heavy expenses of staging the race. One, Clermont-Ferrand, happened to be, and still is, the home of the Michelin tire factories. Monsieur Michelin turned out to be the most generous of the possible supporters. Thus the last of the historic Gordon Bennetts took place on July 5, 1905, over four laps of a wild, 85.35-mile course through the primitive and unique volcano country of the Auvergne Mountains. Clermont-Ferrand, 250 miles south of Paris and halfway between Lyons and Limoges, is its portal.

The people of the region, above all the Sports Association of the Automobile Club of Auvergne in Clermont-Ferrand, never forgot the two thrilling weeks of the Gordon Bennett and its elimination trials and, in 1957, took action to revive that tradition. In May of that year the Association went to work on its five-mile "baby Nürburgring." Two-thirds of the distance consisted of old roads and trails that had to be widened and resurfaced, and the remaining third had to be built from scratch. This was no relatively simple Reims-type task; it was real mountain-highway engineering. The track climbs and descends over a vertical range of 600 feet and its grades are as steep as ten percent. It has fifty-one curves, twenty-six of which have radii of 330 to 1000 feet and twenty-four of which have less than a 330-foot radius. On July 27, 1958, the smoothly asphalted, 30-foot wide circuit welcomed a crowd of 60,000 to its first race. Its creators took well-earned pride in having produced an

Clermont-Ferrand. The main straightaway. The setting is in one of France's most beautiful mountain regions.

arena that was an equally telling test of both men and machines.

Clermont-Ferrand is a superb course, set in magnificently savage country. Fine mountains loom all around, the forest greenery is rich, and the view is inspiring. The Association had built an absolutely outstanding mousetrap and the world beat a willing path to its door.

During its first year of operation Clermont-Ferrand was included as one of the racing sections of the formidable and prestigious *Tour de France,* a flat-out race over vast distances that calls itself a rally. In 1959, Clermont-Ferrand was gobbled up as an ideal stage for the French Motorcycle Grand Prix, counting toward the two-wheel world championship. Then a major Formula Two race was added to its calendar. It drew top entries and was won by Moss. In 1960, an important international sports-car race was inaugurated there.

When 1965 rolled around, the circuit was in magnificent condition. It was a nonprofit operation, having been created for the good of the sport and for the good of this important tourist area. All proceeds had

been poured into permanent structures and general improvements to the circuit. Thus it was ready for the honor the ACF had promised it: the French Grand Prix, to be held there on the sixtieth anniversary of the final Gordon Bennett Cup Race. Even Georges Pompidou, prime minister of the Republic, was on hand for the occasion. And so, of course, was GP racing's entire cast of stars.

The race was spectacular but in no way sensational. Solid professionals found themselves immediately at home, and the less durable cars and less skillful drivers were quickly sorted out by natural process. Jim Clark motored competently and serenely to victory, while fellow-Scot Jackie Stewart placed second. Surtees, who had won the motorcycle GP there in 1959, fought his way to third place although his Ferrari was lame.

Clermont-Ferrand is another candidate for the title of "most beautiful automotive circuit in the world." Its immediate setting at over 2500 feet above sea level is as pleasing as the surrounding mountainous country is majestically impressive. Hills and knolls everywhere provide very safe watching, often with a range of vision of a mile and a half and more. The wild beauty of the *Volcans de France* region makes it a haven for vacationers. It contains eight hundred hotels of all sorts, more than five hundred rustic lodging places, and forty camping sites. It is an unspoiled part of France, where the vanishing art of French cooking at its best still flourishes *and* costs very little. The circuit is a telling test course, and it was here that Goodyear conducted some of its most decisive tests when making its rewarding entry into the Grand Prix field in 1965.

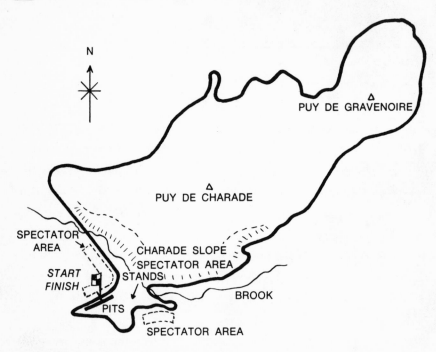

CIRCUIT LENGTH	50.0 miles
RACE DISTANCE	40 laps–200.2 miles, 1965
LAP RECORD	90.53 MPH (race). Clark, Lotus-Climax, 1965
ORGANIZERS	Association Sportive de l'Automobile Club d'Auvergne, 22, rue Blatin, Clermont-Ferrand, France
MONTH	Normally in June

58

Clermont-Ferrand. Much of the course lies on twisting, hilly terrain.

Le Mans—The Bugatti Circuit

The town of Le Mans, about 120 miles southwest of Paris, staged its first Grand Prix race in 1906. It was on its Sarthe Circuit that Jimmy Murphy drove a Duesenberg to victory in 1921 in the first post-World-War-I GP. That exploit was the first European victory for an American driver. It also was the first for an American car.

In 1923 the local organizing club, the *Automobile Club de l'Ouest* (ACO), held the first of its *grandes épreuves d'endurance*, the crushing twenty-four-hour test of men and machines which remains today one of the world's greatest speed contests. In 1967 an American car-driver team triumphed for the second time in European history when Dan Gurney and A. J. Foyt won Le Mans' 24 Hours in a Mk. 4 Ford.

This historic course is 8.36 miles long and most of it runs over public roads that are closed during racing to all other use; but the section of the circuit on which all of its really superb permanent structures stand is the property of the ACO. Here, for years, the club has hoped to create a road circuit on which GP races could be held without immobilizing a good hundred square miles of countryside.

The plan crystallized and work on "the Little Circuit" began early in 1964. At its heart lay the ACO's *Musée de l'Automobile*, the finest automotive museum in France. Thoughts naturally turned to history, and the club decided to name its new circuit after the greatest single figure in French racing annals. Italian-born Ettore Bugatti had begun building high-performance thoroughbreds in France in 1903. Although he had died in 1947, his legend lived on in pure glory. *Le Circuit Bugatti* could not have been given a nobler name.

With a half-century of top-level racing experience behind it the ACO could have done an excellent job of engineering its own new circuit. Instead it called on an even more highly qualified authority, Charles Deutsch. Deutsch is chief engineer of France's Department of Bridges and Roads. He is also the designer of Deutsch-Bonnet and C. D. racing and sports cars, and is a highly experienced competition driver in his own right.

The terrain which Deutsch had to work with — the ACO's own property — is the most interesting on the otherwise nearly dead-level "Big Circuit." It starts just at the end of the long, concrete pits, climbs uphill past the immense grandstands, climbs still higher beyond them, makes a fast, sweeping curve that takes it under the historic Dunlop Bridge, then makes a right-hand hairpin just before reaching the "Big Circuit's" esses. From this point it works its way downhill through a series of very tight corners and one sweeping curve, after which it rejoins the "Big Circuit" on the main straight. There are bleachers at each of the tight corners in addition to the permanent grandstands, which face the pits. The infield is handsomely landscaped and contains a large "village" where all manner of refreshments are available.

The course is sinuous and, from the standpoint of lap speeds, has much in common with Zandvoort. It was designed to be, among other things, a proving ground for manufacturers and a training school for drivers of both racing and touring cars. The design of the track has been criticized for being better suited to these uses than it is to straightforward, all-out road racing. Certainly, acrobatic skills at the wheel and sheer driving virtuosity are at a premium here. But the course is far from being one long slalom; its longest straight measures 4600 feet.

The Bugatti Circuit was completed in April 1965 and the ACO, after having hosted a number of Formula Two and Three events there, held its first Formula One race of the post-World-War-II era. It took place on July 2, 1967, counted for the championship, and . . . hardly anyone attended.

The major reason was simple enough: the super-spectacular twenty-four-hour classic had taken place just three weeks before. It had attracted well over 300,000 spectators, most of whom were still recovering from the round-the-clock experience. Fewer than 15,000 returned to witness

61

the GP.

Fifteen cars came to the starting line. Honda stayed away and Ferrari sent just one machine. The exciting and fast new Ford-Cosworth Lotuses of Clark and Hill, the Eagles of Gurney and McLaren, and the Ferrari of Chris Amon all ran out of reliability. Brabham and Hulme had the race to themselves. Only seven of the original starters finished, and third-place Jackie Stewart came in over a lap behind the leaders.

It was just not a good weekend for machines at Le Mans. Nor was it for the ACO which, in spite of its decades of experience, had to take a costly new lesson in racing management.

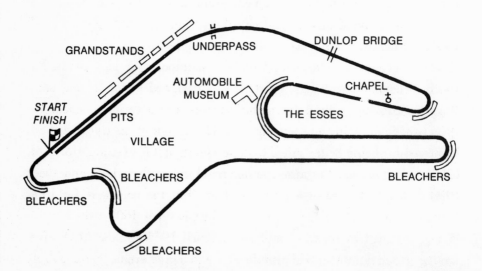

CIRCUIT LENGTH	2.71 miles
RACE DISTANCE	219.2 miles
LAP RECORD	102.29 MPH (race). G. Hill, Ford-Cosworth Lotus
ORGANIZERS	Automobile Club de l'Ouest, Le Mans
MONTH	Normally in July

THE GRAND PRIX OF FRANCE

YEAR	DRIVER	CAR	WINNING SPEED MPH	CIRCUIT
1950	Fangio	Alfa Romeo	104.83	Reims
1951	Fangio	Alfa Romeo	110.97	Reims
1952	Ascari	Ferrari	80.14	Rouen (F2)
1953	Hawthorn	Ferrari	113.65	Reims (F2)
1954	Fangio	Mercedes-Benz	115.67	Reims
1956	Collins	Ferrari	122.29	Reims
1957	Fangio	Maserati	100.02	Rouen
1958	Hawthorn	Ferrari	125.46	Reims
1959	Brooks	Ferrari	127.44	Reims
1960	Brabham	Cooper	132.19	Reims
1961	Baghetti	Ferrari	119.84	Reims
1962	Gurney	Porsche	101.89	Rouen
1963	Clark	Lotus	125.31	Reims
1964	Gurney	Brabham	108.90	Rouen
1965	Clark	Lotus	89.22	Clermont-Ferrand
1966	Brabham	Brabham-Repco	136.89	Reims
1967	Brabham	Brabham-Repco	98.90	Le Mans
1968	Ickx	Ferrari	100.50	Rouen

Bugatti Circuit. Bugatti Circuit shares same start-finish line and main straightaway with the Le Mans sports car course. Shown here is the Miles/Hulme Ford in 1966.

The Grand Prix of Germany

Nürburgring

The first Englishman to race at Nürburgring was Sir Henry Birkin, in a 4.5-liter Bentley in 1928. He described it as, "without hesitation, the finest road circuit in the world." The Nürburgring has been improved considerably since then, and Tim Birkin's opinion has been echoed universally. The Ring is a triumph of what it was intended to be. It is legendary in the racing world.

The first major automotive race in Germany was the Kaiser Prize of 1907. It was run over a short, for that epoch, 73-mile mountainous circuit that had its start and finish at Bad Homburg, in the Taunus country near Frankfurt.

This 292-mile contest was run on the Gordon Bennett pattern and drew ninety-two entries from all over Europe. It left a lasting impression on young people in Germany; and strong efforts were made to establish racing there on an enduring basis and to create a permanent circuit for this purpose. But the German automotive industry yawned at the idea and soon the country was so engrossed in the militarization preceding World War I that the idea had to be shelved for many years.

Germany's first postwar automobile race was organized in 1922 at Cologne. It took place there because of the strong enthusiasm for motor sports of the city's mayor, Dr. Konrad Adenauer. It was also due to the enterprise and sporting spirit of the regional branch of the *Allgemeinen Deutschen Automobil-Club* (ADAC). The success of the first race immediately led the local club to make it an annual feature called the *Eifelrennen*, or Eifel Races, the "Eifel" being the name of the whole

Nürburgring. Among the amenities of the main straightaway is the circuit's own hotel.

region, which is dominated by the once-volcanic Eifel Mountains in the extreme west of Germany.

Dr. Adenauer gave strong official support to this program. It flourished and the old dream of a fine, permanent racing circuit was revived. In 1924, a local group came forward with a plan for a Monza-type speedway-plus-road-circuit, to be built on and around a nearby golf course. The club felt that something better and more original than this should be possible and launched a contest in an effort to discover it.

Herr Hans Weidenbrüke of Bonn had the winning idea. He had spent

Nürburgring. The start-finish area from the air. Excellent garage areas are in foreground at left.

months prowling the country roads and wagon ruts that joined a circle of villages in the mountains around the ruins of ancient Nürburg Castle. This, properly paved, he told the Cologne club late in 1924, could be one of the world's greatest proving grounds for passenger cars, racing cars, and drivers. Club members trekked back into the mountains, explored the terrain, and agreed. On January 19, 1925, the local ADAC branch created a special committee, the mission of which was to make the dream a reality.

Of course, the club had no money. In fact, there was hardly any money in Germany. But there were more than six million unemployed. The special committee schemed.

By April 15, 1925, the committee had hammered out accords with all the communities involved and stood in the presence of the Minister of Public Works in Berlin. It proposed the construction of its circuit as an unemployment relief project to be financed by the national government. In exchange the club would sign a contract guaranteeing to stage four races per year and to reimburse the government, with interest, from the hoped-for proceeds. Adenauer's continuing support helped bureaucracy to move with the rarest speed. Within twelve days, work had commenced on The Ring and for the next two years it provided employment for up to three thousand men.

Racing began on The Ring with the German Grand Prix on June 18, 1927, and since that day its history has been an almost unbroken succession of truly classic contests in the grandest manner and on a heroic scale. In addition to being GP racing's finest arena it is equally superb and uniquely challenging as an arena for sports cars, touring cars, Grand Prix motorcycles, and even for racing bicycles.

The 14.1-mile course is noted for its 176 turns per lap. It climbs and drops over a vertical range of 1041 feet, has downgrades as steep as 11 percent and upgrades that approach 18 percent. All of this means, of course, that drivers get a workout here that they get nowhere else. Naturally it is not a fast course. In spite of its tortuous nature and because of the smoothness of its blacktop pavement it is relatively easy on tires. It is famous for its slight humps, over which cars become momentarily airborne; the faster the car the more of these bumps the driver discovers. It is famous for rain falling on one part of the course and not on others. It is the ultimate "driver's circuit," and its race organization is impeccable.

From the spectator's standpoint it is possible to find fault with The Ring. First, since the cars pass only once every nine minutes or so there is a good deal of time during a race when there is only the scenery to

Nürburgring. The circuit lies in thickly forested mountainous country.

watch. Second, the main grandstand and spectator area is on the dullest part of the course, its main straightaway. But since there is room on the circuit for about 400,000 spectators (300,000 is a normal GP turnout), one has no end of choices of vantage points.

The evolution of GP car design and driving skill is clearly reflected in its lap records. The fastest lap before World War II was Hermann Lang's in a 3-liter, supercharged Mercedes-Benz at 85.71 MPH. It stood unbroken until 1956, when Fangio achieved 87.27 in a 2.5-liter Ferrari.

The following year he got his 250F Maserati around in 91.08, a record that most experts predicted would last for years.

But in 1958 Moss turned 92.42 in a 2.5 Vanwall. In 1961 Phil Hill did 94.36 in a 1.5-liter Ferarri. Then in 1962 Surtees, in a similar car, extended the record to 96.81 and in 1964 pushed it to 98.30. It remained for Jim Clark to break the 100 MPH mark in 1965.

The Ring lies in one of the most beautiful parts of one of the world's most beauty-blessed regions, where the visitor should try to spend as much time as possible. It is very close to such cities as Cologne, Bonn, Koblenz, and Düsseldorf, and to the borders of Luxembourg and Belgium. Many fine scenic roads lead to The Ring and there are excellent tourist accommodations in hospitable, delightful towns and villages throughout the whole of this large and almost fantastically picturesque land of the Eifel. Camping facilities are virtually boundless.

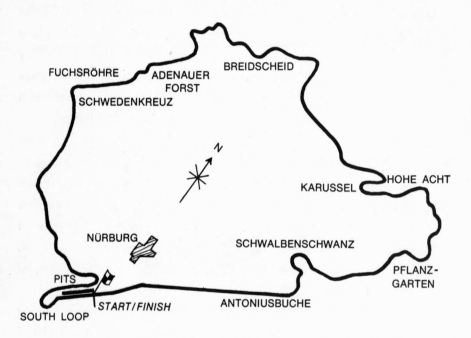

CIRCUIT LENGTH	14.1 miles
RACE DISTANCE	15 laps–211.5 miles, 1966
LAP RECORD	103.15 MPH (race). Gurney, Eagle-Weslake, 1967
ORGANIZERS	Nürburgring GmbH, 5489 Nürburgring/Eifel, Germany
MONTH	Normally in August

Avus

There is no doubt that in the Nürburgring Germany has the finest Grand Prix circuit in the world. Perhaps it is only fair that she should also have the worst. In any case, she has it, in the Avus, the world's longest drag strip. Still, the chicken-bone or rubber-band shaped Avus also is the world's fastest GP circuit, if one can take it seriously as such. But this has happened rarely — only in 1926 for the German GP; in 1954 for the insignificant GP of Berlin (the German GP continued to take place at The Ring); and then in 1959 for the German GP once more. Why the Avus was selected on this occasion is obscure, but political motives were hinted at by the press. This long ribbon of dead-straight pavement is one of the seams in the political football that is divided Berlin.

This stretch of divided highway was constructed as a toll road, running from Berlin to Potsdam, shortly after World War I. It was used as a racing circuit in 1921 and consisted of two 6-mile sections of parallel pavement joined by a hairpin at each end. It is driven counterclockwise, Indianapolis style, and the same rule of the road applies: "Stand on it and turn left." This is not to say that it does not require skill to drive, but the skill required is of a very limited sort. The Avus track has its special dangers, particularly when it is wet.

The Avus GP was instituted in 1931 and between 1933 and 1937 it was a spectacular showcase for the big German cars of that era. In 1937 the Berlin end of the "circuit" was equipped with a brick-paved, 300-foot-radius curve with steep, 43-degree banking. This popularly known "wall of death" permitted drivers to make the loop with very little lifting of the throttle, thus in the minds of many reducing one of the last vestiges of skill demanded by the Avus. But it enabled Luigi Fagioli, in a fully streamlined Auto Union in 1937, to lap the course at a world-stupefying 174 MPH.

Following the war the *Avusrennen*, or the Avus races, consisted of

71

The Avus. The steeply banked north curve leads to an immense "drag strip" straightaway. Arrows, above, mark where drivers have crashed.

minor events, mainly for sports cars. The first Formula One event, the Berlin GP in 1954, was ignored by Ferrari and Maserati and resolved itself into a demonstration of speed by Mercedes-Benz, Fangio creating a postwar lap record of 137.74 MPH. And then, for some reason, in 1959 the German GP was shifted from The Ring to the Avus.

A heavy pall was cast over the big race by the sports-car event of the preceding day. There was rain and popular French champion Jean Behra spun his Porsche at full speed on the wet bricks of the high banking and was killed.

This time the turnout of GP entries was excellent, and the Avus grandstands and public enclosures were filled to their limit of about 60,000 spectators. American drivers attended in abundance: Masten Gregory, Dan Gurney, Phil Hill, and Harry Schell. The GP was run in two heats of thirty laps each, final finishing positions being determined by the combined results of the two. Gregory, in a Cooper, was hailed for his relentless, inspired, and heroic pursuit of the Ferraris, which nevertheless took the first three places, driven by Tony Brooks, Gurney, and Hill. There was nothing really memorable about the race other than the reliability of the four cars that succeeded in going the entire distance at speeds that were unheard of in modern GP racing. And there was Hans Hermann's incredible crash. As he hit his BRM's brakes on approaching the south hairpin at about 160 MPH a section of hydraulic tubing broke and the car crashed into the haybales. It flipped repeatedly and was smashed to rubble. But Hermann, by a miracle, was thrown onto the track, from which he picked himself up with only light injuries.

The experience cured drivers and car owners of any enthusiasm they might have felt for the track, and the German GP was returned to the Nürburgring where it is likely to, and should, stay.

The Avus. The south curve, not banked, is the second of the circuit's two turns.

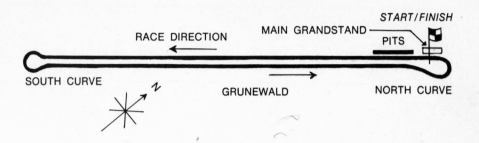

CIRCUIT LENGTH	5.16 miles
RACE DISTANCE	60 laps–309.42 miles, 1959
LAP RECORD	174 MPH (race). Luigi Fagioli, 6-liter Type C Auto Union, 1937
	149.14 MPH (race). Brooks, 2.5-liter Ferrari, 1959
ORGANIZERS	Rennstrecke von Avus, Martinstr. 24, Bonn, Germany
MONTH	Normally in August

THE GRAND PRIX OF GERMANY

YEAR	DRIVER	CAR	WINNING SPEED MPH	CIRCUIT
1951	Ascari	Ferrari	83.76	Nürburgring
1952	Ascari	Ferrari	82.20	Nürburgring F2
1953	Farina	Ferrari	83.89	Nürburgring F2
1954	Fangio	Mercedes-Benz	82.77	Nürburgring
1956	Fangio	Ferrari	85.62	Nürburgring
1957	Fangio	Maserati	88.82	Nürburgring
1958	Brooks	Vanwall	90.31	Nürburgring
1959	Brooks	Ferrari	143.35	Avus
1961	Moss	Lotus	92.34	Nürburgring
1962	G. Hill	BRM	80.28	Nürburgring
1963	Surtees	Ferrari	95.83	Nürburgring
1964	Surtees	Ferrari	96.57	Nürburgring
1965	Clark	Lotus	99.79	Nürburgring
1966	Brabham	Brabham-Repco	86.75	Nürburgring
1967	Hulme	Brabham-Repco	101.47	Nürburgring

The Grand Prix of Holland

Zandvoort

Holland has a long and rich history of motorcycle racing but the first automobile race — for touring cars — did not take place there until 1939. It was to be run on the streets of the town of Zandvoort, about 25 miles north of The Hague and half that distance from Amsterdam. Naturally the experienced officers of the Dutch Motorcycle Federation were asked to help organize the historic event. When they saw Zandvoort's wilderness of sand dunes they immediately saw the possibilities for a fine permanent circuit on private ground. They went to the burgomaster, Mynheer van Alphen, and offered to bring racing to the town if the town would foot the bill for a circuit.

"Forget it," he said. "We have no money, not even enough to buy the rubble for a roadbed."

The Federation men did not forget it, even when the war and the Germans came. The invaders demolished thirty-seven hotels and more than six hundred houses along the seafront to make rubble for their Atlantic Wall. At this time the motorcycle men went back to the burgomaster. One of them, Piet Nortier, tells the story this way:

We went and told him that if rubble was a problem, it wasn't now. "I could not agree with you more," this clever man said. "I have been thinking along the same lines and I already have a plan worked out. Let me see what I can do."

He went directly to the German commanding officer and said, "Perhaps you've heard that there's a war on?"

Of course. He knew.

77

Zandvoort. Sand dunes surrounding the circuit are natural grandstands.

"*And you are absolutely certain that you are going to win this war?*"

Of course!

"*Then, when you have won this war, you'll need a parade ground for celebrating your victory!*"

Oh, that would be grand!

"*That has been our thinking,*" *said the burgomaster,* "*and we have picked out the perfect spot, we think, and are prepared to build the parade ground for you. I have a group of enthusiasts who are ready to tackle the job.*"

78

The Grand Prix of Holland

That, precisely, is how we were able to start building our circuit during the war. That is how a great many of Zandvoort's men escaped being sent to labor camps in Germany. And this is why its official name is the Circuit van Zandvoort — Burgemeester van Alphen.

The foundation of the circuit was completed in 1945, but it lay idle until early 1948 when the new burgomaster, Dr. van Fenema, managed to get a road surface laid in time for the Zandvoort GP in August, 1949. The following year Zandvoort's premier event acquired the title of the Grand Prix of Holland, and in 1952 this race was granted world championship status.

Zandvoort is an extremely interesting circuit, both for drivers and spectators. From the single large grandstand about two-thirds of the course is visible and the dunes everywhere provide natural box seats. There is a none-too-large garage area for competitors, and fine new pits were built in 1966. At the same time the main straight was widened to 70 feet — wider than Le Mans, for example. Since the 2.3-mile course is lapped in just over one and a half minutes there are few dull moments during practice and during the race.

This is a medium-speed circuit, having just one short straight and twelve corners, most of which can be taken at from 80 to 100 MPH. Several of these follow each other in quick sequence, making up a series of rapid, challenging esses. A pair of hairpins with a tricky jog between them helps to make this what is commonly known as a drivers' course. It is one of the better circuits for the testing and development of all types of cars and automotive products; and Honda of Japan used it for its GP test circuit in 1965. The asphalt surface is excellent but tire wear has been medium to severe, depending upon the amount of sand blown onto the pavement, making it abrasive as well as slippery. This annoyance is

79

Zandvoort. Direction of the circuit's second turn gives the impression that the race is run counterclockwise, which it is not.

being brought under increasing control by planting the dunes with grass and elm trees each autumn.

Zandvoort enjoys the reputation of being one of the world's safest motor-racing circuits. An important reason for this is the double — and in some cases triple — chain-link fencing surrounding the course. It catches the cars when they run out of road; and they usually stay right-side up and suffer minimum damage.

The setting here is beautiful, right on the North Sea's edge. It is within easy cruising distance of two great cities. The two coastal access roads are not wide but they still are very adequate to handle the maximum gate of about 50,000 spectators; there are not many circuits in the world

where you can step into your car and drive straight off immediately after a major race. You can do this normally at Zandvoort.

Zandvoort is extremely well maintained and operated, which is to be expected since its manager since 1949 has been John Hugenholtz. This prominent figure in international racing is the world's leading designer of automotive road circuits. His creations stretch from Japan to Oregon and from Finland to Spain. Zandvoort hosts a multitude of speed events in addition to the Dutch GP, is open to the public on most nonrace days, and enjoys about three hundred operational days per year.

The date of the annual Dutch GP has been changed considerably over the summer months. For 1967 it was held during the first week in June where, comfortably insulated against the preceding tulip season and the mass migrations to the beaches which follow a short while later, it may

Zandvoort. Fine modern pits face the main grandstand.

have come to rest on the calendar. This is an ideal time for finding hotel accommodations locally, and camping space is plentiful.

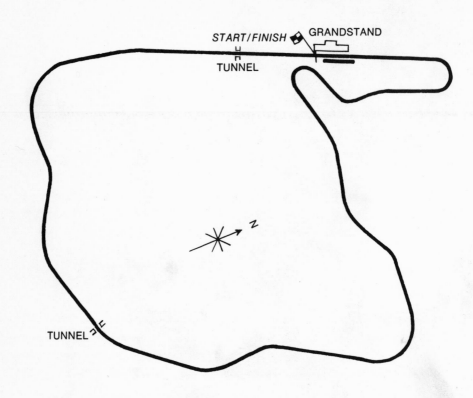

CIRCUIT LENGTH	2.604 miles
RACE DISTANCE	90 laps—234.36 miles
LAP RECORD	106.50 MPH (race). Clark, Lotus-Ford, 1967
ORGANIZERS	Circuit van Zandvoort, Zandvoort, Holland
MONTH	Normally in June

THE GRAND PRIX OF HOLLAND
(Zandvoort Circuit)

YEAR	DRIVER	CAR	WINNING SPEED MPH
1952	Ascari	Ferrari	81.15–F2
1953	Ascari	Ferrari	81.04–F2
1955	Fangio	Mercedes-Benz	89.65
1958	Moss	Vanwall	93.95
1959	Bonnier	BRM	93.46
1960	Brabham	Cooper	96.27
1961	von Trips	Ferrari	96.21
1962	G. Hill	BRM	95.44
1963	Clark	Lotus	97.53
1964	Clark	Lotus	98.02
1965	Clark	Lotus	100.87
1966	Brabham	Brabham-Repco	100.04
1967	Clark	Lotus-Ford	104.44

85

The Grand Prix of Italy

Everyone calls the circuit "Monza," but its correct name is the National Autodrome. In every sense it is one of the most important racing installations in the world.

The Grand Prix of Italy was originated by the Automobile Club of Milan and was held at Brescia, a long way from the northern Italian industrial metropolis. The AC of Milan fought for a circuit closer to home, and early in 1922 was granted permission to create a racing plant on part of the grounds of the vast Royal Park at Monza, a nearby suburb.

At that period the Indianapolis "500" was the most important race in the world, and the Italians studied the greatest of American circuits with care. They adopted its high speed oval, which they then tied into an interesting road course. The total distance around was 6.21 miles and the layout was such that the cars passed the grandstand twice during each lap, making for wonderful watching.

It was on February 26, 1922, that Vincenzo Lancia and Felice Nazzaro — both great racing drivers who had become car manufacturers — laid the track's first paving stone. Just 110 days later the great circuit was in operation and the Italian Grand Prix had a new home.

But Monza meant much more. It immediately became the home of Italy's motorcycle Grand Prix. Year after year, until today, it has been the scene of almost countless other racing events and record attempts. Throughout its history it has served as a test track and proving ground for industry. The influence that Monza has had on the traditional excellence of Italian high-performance cars has been immense, and manufacturers and record-seekers from other countries are indebted to it as well.

Monza was designed to provide excellent protection for spectators, including the provision of husky guard-walls in critical areas. But during

Monza. The start of the 1954 GP of Italy, seen from in front of the main grand-stand.

the Grand Prix of Europe (which was initiated at Monza in 1923), a large crowd poured beyond one of these walls just as Emilio Materassi lost control of his Talbot. The driver and twenty spectators were killed. The national press had a field day with this disaster and heaped blame on the police of the town of Monza, who were held responsible for crowd control at the Autodrome. To this day the Monza police have a well-deserved reputation for being the most nervous, edgy, and unpleasant in the entire racing world.

In 1929 Achille Varzi (Alfa Romeo) and Alfieri Maserati (Maserati) lapped the circuit at over 200 KPH (122 MPH) for the first time in its

Monza. The famous banked high-speed course is rarely used today. Tony Bettenhausen, No. 27, set the still-unbroken lap record here in 1957.

history. As a result of this "excessive" speed, plus the Materassi tragedy, authorities demanded that the circuit be slowed down, and in 1930 its length was reduced to 4.26 miles. Then in 1933 three drivers shot off the high-speed oval and were killed. The speedway section was abandoned and finally was demolished in 1939.

During World War II Monza was used as a proving ground for industry until 1942, when it was requisitioned by the Italian Army. Later it was taken over by the German Army, which used it as a base for vehicles and manpower until the Allied victory.

The entire plant remained in excellent condition throughout the war years, after which it was taken over by the Americans and British as a dump for surplus war materiél. This caused a good deal of damage to the park, but the destruction reached its peak when General Mark Clark staged a display of American military might for the natives' benefit. A massive parade of tanks around the circuit ruined its surface.

The military forces withdrew from Monza at the end of 1947 and the materiél dump was cleared early in 1948. The AC of Milan went to work immediately on the restoration of the entire installation and resumed racing there in October of that year. Monza's first postwar Italian GP was held in 1949.

In June of 1955 Pierre Levegh's Mercedes-Benz crashed into the crowd during the 24-hour race at Le Mans, causing the death of about eighty people. The disaster came very close to putting a permanent end to automobile racing in many parts of the world. The Grands Prix of France, Germany, Spain, and Switzerland were canceled. The Swiss government abolished motor racing for all time and the American Automobile Association disbanded its Contest Board. The Italians not only went racing as usual, they built a new ultra-high-speed oval into the Monza circuit. This oval is 2.65 miles in circumference, which, if flat and with an impossible coefficient of friction of 100 percent, would permit a theoretical top speed of about 125 MPH. But the new Monza oval was banked to a maximum steepness of 38° 40′, making possible lap speeds approaching 200 MPH. The all-time lap record on this speedway section of the circuit was set in 1958 during qualifying trials for the "Monzanapolis" 500-mile race. The driver was Tony Bettenhausen, his car an American Novi, and his average speed was 177.047 MPH.

The combined road course and oval have a length of 6.214 miles. After the Italian GP of 1961 the oval was abandoned for road-racing use for several reasons. One is that the joints between the concrete slabs of the pavement are somewhat uneven and rough. This was tolerable until GP cars began becoming increasingly light and fragile. Another is that the higher the speed on a banked curve, the higher the loading on the suspension system. This did not mix well with recent engineering trends, and thus a most fabulous course has been lost to the sport.

Monza is very handy to the great city of Milan and is best reached by automobile. There are hotels in the pleasant town of Monza but these are always crowded at race time and most visitors stay in Milan. The immense park in which the circuit is located is beautifully forested and has a fine camping area close to the track. There is a good restaurant in the track village and an ordinary one under the main grandstand. The September weather normally ranges from warm to very hot and rain is not rare. Monza recently was given the Grand Prix Drivers' Association's award for safety — for drivers and spectators.

CIRCUIT LENGTH   3.6 miles
RACE DISTANCE   68 laps–244.8 miles, 1966
LAP RECORD   145.33 MPH (race). Clark, Lotus-Ford, 1967

ORGANIZERS   Autodromo Nazionale, Monza, Italy

MONTH   Normally in September

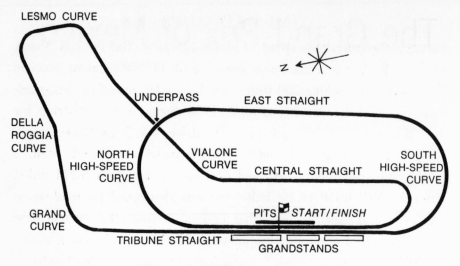

THE GRAND PRIX OF ITALY
(Monza Circuit)

YEAR	DRIVER	CIRCUIT	CAR	WINNING SPEED MPH
1950	Farina	F	Alfa Romeo	109.63
1951	Ascari	F	Ferrari	115.53
1952	Ascari	F	Ferrari	109.80 F2
1953	Fangio	F	Maserati	110.69 F2
1954	Fangio	F	Mercedes-Benz	111.99
1955	Fangio	G	Mercedes-Benz	128.42
1956	Moss	G	Maserati	129.73
1957	Moss	H	Vanwall	120.27
1958	Brooks	H	Vanwall	121.21
1959	Moss	H	Cooper	124.38
1960	P. Hill	G	Ferrari	132.06
1961	P. Hill	G	Ferrari	130.08
1962	G. Hill	H	BRM	123.62
1963	Clark	H	Lotus	127.74
1964	Surtees	H	Ferrari	127.77
1965	Stewart	H	BRM	130.47
1966	Scarfiotti	H	Ferrari	135.93
1967	Surtees	H	Honda	140.54

The Grand Prix of Mexico

Magdalena Mixhuca Circuit

When this excellent circuit was completed in 1961 by the Mexican government's Social Security Administration it formed part of a "sports city" that was being prepared for the 1968 Olympic Games. The 7,500-foot-high setting of Mexico City and its surrounding valley is magnificent and is dominated by the snow-covered volcanoes of Iztaccihuatl and of Popocatepetl, which towers more than 10,000 feet above the valley floor. That a road-racing circuit was included in the Olympic community was probably due largely to the personal automotive enthusiasm of Adolfo López Mateos, president of Mexico from 1958 through 1964.

Because Mexico has the highest standard of living in all of Latin America plus an outstanding architectural tradition, Mexico's Magdalena Mixhuca Circuit was expected to be something out of the ordinary. No one was surprised when it turned out to be one of the best-designed and best-equipped racing plants in the world. It resembles Riverside Raceway and, in a less ambitious way, the Buenos Aires race course in that several alternative courses are available within the 3.10-mile periphery track. It is the outer course on which Formula One events are contested.

It is entirely surrounded by chain-link fencing, has a fine permanent grandstand, garage area, and pits, plenty of clean toilets and running water, and is handsomely landscaped. The circuit is tight and twisty despite the fact that it has three straights, one about a mile long. It has five S-bends, three of which follow one another in quick sequence. It has fourteen highly varied bends and curves in all, and is a trying and challenging course to drive. It is at least equally trying for engine mechanics who lack experience in high-altitude carburetion. All cars suffer a loss

93

Mexico City. This aerial photo shows the main grandstand and superb garage area.

in engine output of about 25 percent, although it has been noticed that the loss declines with an increased number of cylinders. The eights seem to breathe more freely than the fours, and the twelves better than the eights.

The first Mexican GP — the one that qualified the race for championship status — took place in 1962. During practice, drivers expressed admiration for the course except for its last curve, a half-mile banked turn with such an irregular surface that shift levers had to be held in gear by brute force. It was on this Peraltada Curve that Mexico's best-known driver, Ricardo Rodriguez, lost his life in practice. Ironically, the accident occurred on the eve of All Souls Day, a day which all of Mexico devotes to remembrance of the dead. The loss of the twenty-year-old national hero cast a strange, leaden pall over the race.

The Grand Prix of Mexico

Nevertheless an estimated 100,000 people turned out for Mexico's historic first GP. They listened in utter silence to a eulogy for Rodriguez, and then witnessed the absurdly botched start of the race and its well-policed, well-marshaled development as Clark drove his Lotus to a smooth victory. The FIA agreed to award championship status to the event, providing the Peraltada Curve be resurfaced. This already had been ordered by Mexico's grief-stricken president, along with the renaming of the circuit.

The Mexican organizers, working in cooperation with the organizers of New York's Watkins Glen Grand Prix, assembled an excellent field of twenty-one starters for 1963. Few knew the course as Clark did. He led from start to finish and walked away with the race and the lap record.

In 1964 the race was honored, as always, by the presence of Mexico's president and also by that of the Duke of Edinburgh. The Scottish victory, which the Duke and most others had good reason to expect, was snatched from Clark on the next-to-last lap when Clark's engine failed. Gurney in a Brabham-Climax rushed by to win. This was the race in

Mexico City. The racing circuit is just one of the fine facilities of a modern sports city.

Mexico City. The tight turns are tricky,
and rubber tires imbedded in the pavement are no aid to driver safety.

which Bandini nerfed Graham Hill into a spin, making possible Surtees' second place finish and his first world championship on four wheels.

The next year, 1965, brought more good fortune to the American entries. Richie Ginther won for himself and Honda their first GP victories, and Gurney followed him in second place, again in a Brabham-Climax.

The highlight of the Mexican GP in 1966 was Surtees' win in a 3-liter Cooper-Maserati; it was the first GP victory for one of these cars and Cooper's first in a championship event since 1962. It was repeated in the 1967 South African GP by Ricardo Rodriguez' brother Pedro. While Ginther could place his Honda no better than fourth in the 1966 Mexican race, he set a new lap record for the race and was clocked at 170 MPH on the mile-long straight. Here, in 1967, Denis Hulme clinched the world championship with a fourth-place finish. He and his partner, Jack Brabham, finished the season with just two victories each. Jim Clark's Lotus-Ford win was his fourth for the year.

Mexico City, of course, is one of the tourist capitals of the hemisphere. The circuit is very close to the international airport and is only about a twenty-minute drive from the center of the city. Hotels and motels are everywhere and the autumn weather is usually ideal.

CIRCUIT LENGTH	3.10 miles
RACE DISTANCE	65 laps–201.5 miles
LAP RECORD	103.37 MPH (race). Clark, Lotus-Ford, 1967
ORGANIZERS	Comité Organizador, Gran Premio de México, Lancaster 17, México 6, D. F., México
MONTH	Normally in October

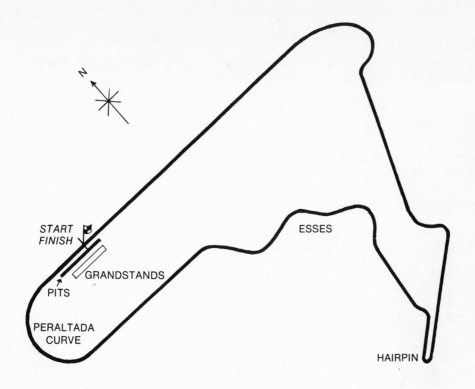

START
FINISH

ESSES

GRANDSTANDS

PITS

PERALTADA
CURVE

HAIRPIN

THE GRAND PRIX OF MEXICO
(Magdalena Autodrome — Mexico City)

YEAR	DRIVER	CAR	WINNING SPEED MPH
1963	Clark	Lotus	93.30
1964	Gurney	Brabham	93.11
1965	Ginther	Honda	94.26
1966	Surtees	Cooper-Maserati	95.78
1967	Clark	Lotus-Ford	101.42

Monaco. Without doubt this is the world's most picturesque road-racing circuit.

The Grand Prix of Monaco

Monaco has a long tradition of hospitality to engines and to speed. In 1900, it became a center for the testing and development of pioneer aircraft. In 1905, the most elegant of the world's *Concours d'Elegance* was initiated at the Casino. During this period Monaco became the speedboat-racing capital of Europe. In 1911 the first of the classic Monte Carlo Rallies was held. Then, in 1929, Anthony Noghès, president of the principality's automobile club, conceived and organized the first Grand Prix of Monaco. The prominent British publication, *The Motor*, commented at the time:

> *One of the most unsuitable circuits ever chosen for a road course will be used for the first Grand Prix of Monaco. There is no doubt that the race is extremely difficult and will produce a winning car of the first class and a truly expert driver. One false move will put the car and driver into the port or into the sea.*

The author of these lines was correct on all counts, yet in 1966 another writer in the same journal could speak of the Grand Prix of Monaco as "the most enjoyable Championship race of the year," which would be hard to deny.

Its setting, of course, is legendary. Monaco starts at the blue Mediterranean's edge and clings to hills and cliffs that sweep to the barren, 3,600-foot summit of majestic Mount Agel. The principality covers only 370 acres but it is so densely packed with buildings that it gives the impression of being a great city. Still, its population is only about 22,500; and of this number fewer than 2,000 are actually citizens of Monaco. France finds it worthwhile to recognize the little princedom, whose happy citizens for some reason are exempt from military service and taxes.

The short, 1.953-mile race course is the world's classic example of the round-the-houses circuit. Because it is in the heart of a building- and skyscraper-jammed civic complex it has probably undergone less change in its history than any other Grand Prix circuit, a fact that makes its year-by-year racing record particularly instructive.

Monaco's start-finish line and dangerously exposed pits are located at the head of the picturesque small harbor which is usually crowded with glittering yachts. No part of the circuit is straight for more than a few feet and there are eleven curves, including two hairpins. Less than half of it is flat and its ups and downs range from sea level to 132 feet above. Curbs, sea walls, a 300-foot-long tunnel and curbside utility poles all contribute to its hazards, not to mention the sea, which borders half the course. Driving 100 laps at Monaco flat out and making no less than 2,000 gear changes in two and a half hours is no easy test of man or machine and is much more fatiguing than racing for longer distances on longer, faster circuits. On them a driver can relax on the straightaways while at Monaco there is not a second's rest. As for machines, Monaco stresses their brakes, transmissions, clutches, steering, and many other parts as no other Grand Prix course can.

Small, light, and nimble cars are suited best to this circuit. The Ferrari 2.4 V6 of 1966 was built specifically for Monaco under the then-new 3-liter formula. Ferrari driver John Surtees was given a 3-liter V12 to drive but had too much power. Lorenzo Bandini, in the smaller, less-powerful Ferrari, set a new lap record and finished second, just 40 seconds behind the winner.

A surprising characteristic of this circuit is that, in spite of all the cornering involved, tire wear is not a problem. The speeds are relatively low, the well-used asphalt is very smooth (and slippery when wet), and

102

Monaco. Round-the-houses racing is exciting and colorful but curbs, power poles, and trees are hazardous.

Goodyear's biggest problem there has been getting its tires "scrubbed" — wearing off the glaze all new tires have when they come out of the mold. Firestone's Bob Martin remarked after the 1966 race, "Our Indianapolis tire works quite well here but at the end of the race we had almost more rubber on the tire than we started with. It seems to pick up worn rubber from the course. You can run here all week and there is just *no* wear on the tire."

Monaco is not popular with builders of racing cars; it is scorned by Ferrari as "a drawing-room racing circuit." It is short, slow, and not like any other Formula One course in the world. Because it is a hard circuit on machinery many builders prefer to run their previous season's cars at Monaco and to save their newest models for the second Grand Prix of the European season, at Zandvoort, a month later.

103

Monaco. Drivers Alberto Ascari and Paul Hawkins have both crashed in the Bay of Monaco. This re-enactment is from the film Grand Prix.

The Grand Prix of Monaco

In spite of its shortcomings Monaco does not have a bad accident
record, generally speaking. But the tragic and, according to many critics,
unnecessary death of Lorenzo Bandini there in 1967 has caused many
of the parties who are most concerned to have serious second thoughts.
Perhaps *The Motor* had a point when, back in 1929, it described Monaco
as "One of the most unsuitable circuits ever. . . ."

THE GRAND PRIX OF MONACO

YEAR	DRIVER	CAR	WINNING SPEED MPH
1950	Fangio	Alfa Romeo	61.33
1955	Trintignant	Ferrari	65.81
1956	Moss	Maserati	64.94
1957	Fangio	Maserati	64.72
1958	Trintignant	Cooper	67.99
1959	Brabham	Cooper	66.71
1960	Moss	Lotus	67.46
1961	Moss	Lotus	70.70
1962	McLaren	Cooper	70.46
1963	G. Hill	BRM	72.43
1964	G. Hill	BRM	73.04
1965	G. Hill	BRM	74.34
1966	Stewart	BRM	76.51
1967	Hulme	Brabham-Repco	75.89

CIRCUIT LENGTH	1.953 miles
RACE DISTANCE	100 laps–244.8 miles
LAP RECORD	78.60 MPH (race). Clark, Lotus-Climax, 2L, 1967
ORGANIZERS	Grand Prix Automobile de Monaco, Monaco
MONTH	Normally in May

THE GRAND PRIX OF MONACO
LAP RECORDS

YEAR	DRIVER	CAR	TIME	SPEED KPH	MPH
1950	Fangio	Alfa Romeo	1m51s	103.135	
1955	Fangio	Mercedes	1m42.4s	110.568	
1956	Fangio	Ferrari	1m44.4s	108.450	
1957	Fangio	Maserati	1m45.6s	107.217	
1958	Hawthorn	Ferrari	1m40.6s	112.547	
1959	Brabham	Cooper	1m40.4s	112.771	
1960	McLaren	Cooper	1m36.2s	117.694	
1961	Ginther	Ferrari	1m36.3s	117.570	
1962	Clark	Lotus	1m35.5s	118.554	
1963	Surtees	Ferrari	1m34.5s	119.809	
1964	G. Hill	BRM	1m33.9s	120.575	
1965	G. Hill	BRM	1m31.7s	123.467	
1966	Bandini	Ferrari	1m29.8s		78.25
1967	Hulme	Brabham-Repco			75.89

NOTE: Since this circuit has remained essentially unchanged throughout its history the changes in its lap records are particularly meaningful.

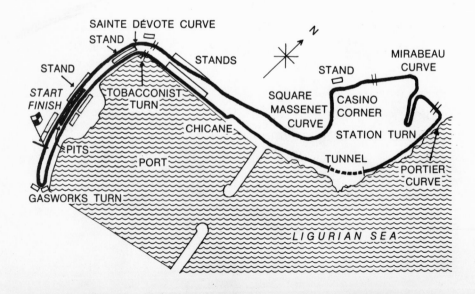

The Grand Prix of Portugal

Oporto—Circuito da Boa Vista

The first Portuguese GP for sports cars was held in Oporto in 1951, and it continued to draw a large field of local entries through 1953. The following year the event was moved to Lisbon, after which it alternated between the two cities. Portugal's first Formula One championship race took place at Oporto in 1958 and was won by a brilliantly consistent Moss, who led in 34 out of the 50 laps. Mike Hawthorn finished almost five minutes behind him. Of the fifteen starters only these two finishers went the entire distance. The course was tough and unknown to most of the drivers.

By the time of the 1960 race at Oporto, tremendous technical development had taken place and twelve of the sixteen entries were able to improve upon Hawthorn's 1958 lap record of 108.74 MPH. It was this race that put the seal on Brabham's championship that year. But Surtees was the sensation of the event. This was his first year in automobile racing, yet at Oporto he led for almost half the race, broke the lap record, and for the first time really revealed his potential to become a champion. And that was the last of the Grands Prix at Oporto.

The 4.65-mile circuit was laid out in the suburbs of the city, most of it running through residential areas. The start-finish line was on the short Esplanada do Rio de Janeiro, bordering the sea. Here the cobblestone pavement was coated with a film of slick asphalt which became like grease when the salt-water mist rolled in. At the end of this very wide straight the cars jolted over streetcar rails, warped 90 degrees to the left around a traffic circle, and then shot down the 1.5-mile Avenida da Boa Vista straight, from which the circuit took its name. After this the road climbed to a very tortuous and dangerously tree-lined 3-mile back-leg,

107

GP of Portugal –Oporto. Stirling Moss leads down the Esplanade in the 1958 Portuguese Grand Prix.

then plunged downhill to the Esplanada. The course had its hazards, including sand that blew onto the pavement from the adjacent beach. But, wrote *Autocar* at the time, "Oporto presents true and realistic road racing conditions, the antithesis of the banked track at Monza. If such conditions are desirable, then Oporto's is an ideal Grand Prix circuit."

It was impossibly rough on the newer GP cars and this is the reason given for its retirement. In 1964 a 1.86-mile road course was established on part of the original circuit but it will never be used for Formula One.

The Grand Prix of Portugal

CIRCUIT LENGTH 4.65 miles

RACE DISTANCE 55 laps–253 miles

LAP RECORD 111.72 MPH (race). Brabham, 2.5-liter Cooper-Climax

ORGANIZERS Automóvil Club de Portugal, rua Rosa Araujo 24, Lisbon, Portugal

MONTH Normally in August

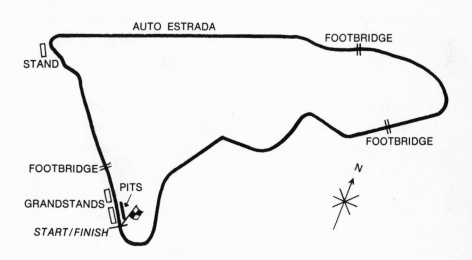

Lisbon—Monsanto Circuit

This "little Nürburgring-type" circuit was laid out in a very large public park in the hills north of the city. It might still be in operation if the flourishing trees had not grown so thick and high that it lost its spectator appeal. Also, part of the course included a section of the main coastal highway, and shutting this artery down for racing purposes was never universally popular.

The variety at Monsanto was popular with drivers and public. Corners ranged from fast, sweeping bends to tight hairpins, most of it twisted up and down hill, but there was a slightly uphill one-mile straight beside the sea that permitted speeds of at least 150 MPH. It was a roller-coaster ride that the drivers enjoyed. The only complaint from them in 1959 concerned holding practice just at day's end and the need to drive against the sunset's glare.

There were sixteen cars in the entry list that year but Moss was in a class entirely by himself. In one of the most authoritative performances of his career, he lapped every car in the race in his Cooper-Climax. American Masten Gregory came in second, a lap behind in a similar car, and his countryman, Dan Gurney, finished third in a Ferrari. Other Americans involved were Harry Schell, fifth; Carrol Shelby, eighth; and Phil Hill, whose Ferrari did not finish. Jack Brabham declared, " I consider this circuit to be one of the most decisive tests in the entire championship," and it was scratched from the calendar.

Portugal has several other excellent racing circuits, including one at Cascais, a delightfully picturesque seaside town just a few miles from Lisbon. Racing on the national level continued here, and serious plans were laid for the resumption of the Formula One GP of Portugal at Cascais in 1967. Then, in the last race of the 1966 season, there was a fatal accident which involved spectators. The public reacted violently —

GP of Portugal — Lisbon. The Monsanto Circuit ran through urban Lisbon and over adjoining highways.

the bull is never killed in Portuguese bullfights — with the result that the Automobile Club of Portugal announced that there would be no International GP in 1967 nor in any other year.

CIRCUIT LENGTH	3.38 miles
RACE DISTANCE	62 laps–210 miles
LAP RECORD	97.23 MPH (race). Moss, 2.5-liter Cooper-Climax
ORGANIZERS	See Oporto table
MONTH	August

111

THE GRAND PRIX OF PORTUGAL

YEAR	DRIVER	CAR	WINNING SPEED MPH	CIRCUIT
1958	Moss	Vanwall	105.03	Oporto
1959	Moss	Cooper	95.32	Lisbon
1960	Brabham	Cooper	109.27	Oporto

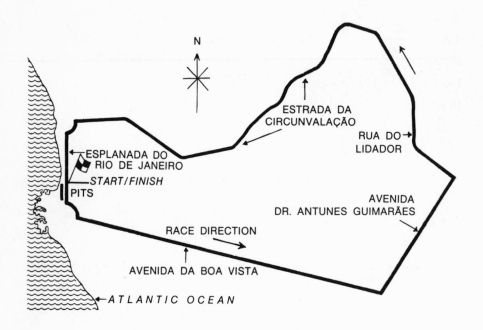

The Grand Prix of South Africa

East London

The first race to be run under the 3-liter Formula One was the South African Grand Prix, which took place at East London on January 1, 1966. The event already had been deleted from the championship calendar for the excellent reason that, except for a single Brabham-Repco (which came within an ace of winning), no 3-liter machines were ready to do battle at that early date.

East London is an industrial city and seaport on the Indian Ocean and its cream-colored sandy beaches make it a popular resort spot as well. Its enthusiastic inhabitants point out that "international Grand Prix racing" had its South African beginnings there back in 1934. That race, called The Border 100, was won by Whitney Straight in his privately owned Maserati, hotly pursued by local driver J. H. Case in a Ford. This modest event was a commercial success, and its organizers applied to the Royal Automobile Club of South Africa for authorization to rechristen it the South African Grand Prix. This was granted, and the race remained as an annual fixture until the outbreak of World War II.

East London's successful pioneering was imitated in 1937 by the organizers of the Rand GP in Johannesburg and the Grosvenor GP in Cape Town. For some obscure reason Auto Union sent Berend Rosemeyer and Ernst von Delius to make a mockery of the British ERA's and Rileys in the Grosvenor that year, and in 1938 and 1939 some top Italian drivers appeared in 1.5-liter Maseratis. Otherwise these races resembled chummy little British club meetings infinitely more than "international Grands Prix." After all, South Africa was a long way south of Timbuktu and the jet transport that would bring it within hours of Europe was far in the future.

113

East London. Sand from the nearby beaches of the Indian Ocean creates an abrasive surface on this resort-area circuit. Last used for the South African Grand Prix of 1966, this course is not expected to be the site of future GP's.

After World War II, several of the old East London racing fans banded together to bring motor racing back to their city. They ran races on its seafront Esplanade from 1951 through 1957, bringing droves of visitors to the community. When they asked their city council to donate a proper road-racing circuit the request was granted with enthusiasm.

The first race was held there in the dead of winter, on July 13, 1959. The organizers looked upon it as an experiment which, if successful, would "bring back" Grand Prix racing to South Africa. A huge crowd turned out to witness the Republic's best handlers of racing cars and motorcycles in action, and Caltex Oil, Ltd. came forward to help finance the big dream: South Africa's first postwar GP.

114

Two such events, both for sports cars, took place in 1960. Then the 1961 Formula One meet qualified East London for the championship. It was won by Clark in the inevitable Lotus at 92.29 MPH. He also set the lap record at 94.18 MPH.

South Africa's first Formula One championship GP took place on December 28, 1962. It was, obviously, the last race of the season, but the world title still hung in the balance. A record crowd of 90,000 thronged the course and saw Clark headed for another certain victory. Then a cheap fiber washer failed, causing the oil leak that deprived Clark of the championship and gave it to Graham Hill.

The 1963 GP of South Africa also was held at the year's end and this time Clark's machine did not betray him. His win had no bearing on the championship, which he had nailed down several races before.

At this point East London's organizers decided that it would be shrewd to shift their Grand Prix a few days ahead, making it the first instead of the last of the season. This meant missing 1964 entirely but the real difference was, after all, one of only a few days. Through this strategy the organizers apparently hoped to attract teams with the newest machines and perhaps to get bumper crops of top entries who, presumably, would be eager to kick off the season with all the championship points they could get. The idea was a failure in 1965, when Clark paraded to another monotonous win, and it was a greater failure in 1966. In 1967 the South African GP was transferred to the Kyalami Circuit at Johannesburg, where it is expected to remain.

The East London circuit lies between the dunes bordering the Indian Ocean and an arc of hills about a mile inland. The course is slightly undulating and falls in the medium-fast bracket. It has eight pronounced bends, two of which are almost hairpins and three of which are extremely fast sweeps. As it is located on the coast it can be very windy, and sand on the track is among its hazards. The pavement is abrasive and the rate of tire wear is high.

Little history has been made at East London but one milestone stands out clearly. It was here, in 1965, that Goodyear made its entry into Formula One racing. It was the beginning of a major revolution in racing technology.

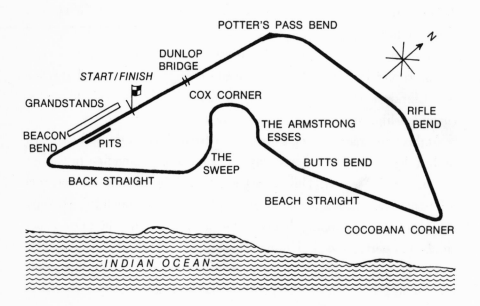

CIRCUIT LENGTH	2.4356 miles
RACE DISTANCE	85 laps–207 miles, 1965
LAP RECORD	103.09 MPH (race). Brabham, Brabham-Repco, 1966
ORGANIZERS	Die S.A. Grand Prix Baan, East London, Union of South Africa
MONTH	Normally in January

Kyalami

Due to their long-standing priority the organizers of East London also are the official, ultimate organizers of Grand Prix racing in South Africa. When it finally became apparent that East London simply did not have a sufficiently large population to support modern Grand Prix racing, other possibilities were considered. The obvious and overwhelming choice was the fine, modern Kyalami Circuit. It is located just a few miles from Johannesburg, South Africa's largest city, which has a population in excess of 1.1 million.

The Kyalami Circuit was built in 1961 by the South African Motor Racing Club, with the strong support of Johannesburg's sportsminded mayor, Dave Marais. The force behind the operation of the circuit is Alex Blignaut, who set its first lap record at the controls of a tractor and disc plow during groundbreaking ceremonies. He has served as director of the circuit and as secretary of the SAMRC ever since.

The new, 2.544-mile arena for the South African Grand Prix lies on gently rolling ground at an elevation of about 6,000 feet, almost as high as Mexico City. The main grandstand, officials' and press tower, start-finish line, and permanent pits are located on the highest point of the course, from which its entire sweep can be viewed. Beyond the pits the main straight makes a deep dip, then rises to meet the first of nine highly varied bends. These include a set of esses, a steep, climbing hairpin, and The Kink, which can be taken at upwards of 120 MPH. Helping to keep drivers on their toes, most of the bends do not have a constant radius and most of them involve blind rises that make it impossible to see the road ahead. With a width of only 24 feet the circuit was unusually narrow until it was widened to 36 feet during the 1967 season. This work brought the total investment in the Kyalami plant to about $390,000.

It is a very prosperous circuit on which as many as ten events are held each year, including the prestigious 9-Hour endurance race sponsored

117

Kyalami. Heat, high altitude and tricky turns combine to make this one of the most demanding of all GP courses. Spectators in the grandstands can see almost the entire circuit.

by the *Rand Daily Mail*. The circuit's grandstands provide covered seating for 8000 spectators, plus open stands for another 10,000. The 1967 Formula One race drew a crowd of 90,000.

Kyalami's first race was a Formula One event held on November 4, 1961, and its first championship Grand Prix took place on January 2, 1967. Only the four local drivers among the eighteen entries in this historic event were accustomed to driving in 100-degree heat, which held the track-level temperature at around 140 degrees. This heat, combined with the very high altitude, helped to eliminate all but eight contestants in what was one of Grand Prix racing's more memorable debacles. As such talents as Jackie Stewart, Graham Hill, Jim Clark, Jo Bonnier, Mike Spence, Jochen Rindt, and Dan Gurney fell by the way, Rhodesian John Love, driving an aged four-cylinder, 2.7-liter Cooper-Climax, moved into the lead on Lap 60. To the thoroughly justifiable wild enthusiasm of the local horde, Love held his lead unchallenged for 14 laps. Then, with only 6 laps to go, his engine began to splutter and he had to pit for fuel. This operation let Pedro Rodriguez' Cooper-Maserati into the lead with a 40-second advantage which Love had been able to trim to only 26 seconds when the checkered flag fell. This was Rodriguez' first championship victory and John Surtees finished third in his first factory drive for Honda of Japan.

Kyalami. Sports cars negotiating Lion Head Bend, one of several fast curves on this course, site of the 1967 South African GP.

CIRCUIT LENGTH	2.544 miles
RACE DISTANCE	80 laps–203.5 miles
LAP RECORD	101.87 MPH (race). Hulme, Brabham-Repco
ORGANIZERS	South African Motor Racing Club, 303 Permanent Bldg., Johannesburg, South Africa
MONTH	Normally in January

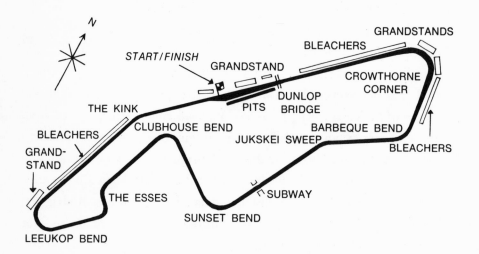

THE GRAND PRIX OF SOUTH AFRICA

YEAR	DRIVER	CAR	WINNING SPEED MPH	
1962	G. Hill	BRM	93.57	East London
1963	Clark	Lotus	95.10	East London
1965	Clark	Lotus	97.97	East London
1967	Rodriguez	Cooper-Maserati	97.90	Kyalami

The Grand Prix of Spain

Barcelona—Pedralbes Circuit

The Spanish appetite for big-time automobile racing got its first satisfaction from the Peña Rhin Grand Prix at Barcelona in 1921. This event for high-performance cars of up to 1.5 liters' displacement continued for just two more years. In 1923, the immortal Tazio Nuvolari finished fifth here, in his first race away from Italian soil.

Ten years later the Peña Rhin GP was revived, this time as an arena for the huge, howling, no-displacement-limit open-formula machines of the thirties. It took place on the roads of the Municipal Park of Montjuich in the heart of the city, one of the most picturesque circuits of that or any era. In 1936, Manuel Anzana's Fascist revolution brought chaos to the Spanish peninsula and put an end to racing there. The winner of the final prewar event in that year was Nuvolari, who managed to outdistance Caracciola's Mercedes with an obsolescent Alfa Romeo.

The Peña Rhin Automobile Club was among the world's first to resume racing after the war and its eighth GP was held on Barcelona's Pedralbes Circuit (public thoroughfares closed to traffic, as before) in October of 1946. It was strictly a hometown affair for the benefit of the lucky owners of prewar Maseratis and such, but it served as a rehearsal for a series of historically important international events which continued for eight more years. Only the races of 1951 and 1954 counted toward the championship.

The 1948 and 1949 Peña Rhin Grands Prix were first-class events in every sense. They drew outstanding fields of cars and drivers from England, France, and Italy, plus crowds in astronomic numbers. All this encouraged the organizers to make their 1950 event a qualifier for a place on the just-created championship calendar. That race was particu-

121

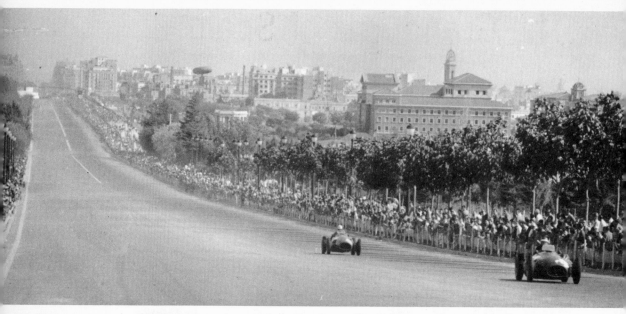

GP of Spain — Barcelona. The last Spanish Grand Prix to be run on Barcelona's Pedralbes Circuit was won by Mike Hawthorn in 1954.

larly memorable as the first GP appearance of the highly promising V16 BRM and as the second appearance of the new 4.5-liter unsupercharged Ferrari. Ascari won the race in one of these machines at 93.93 MPH and Peña Rhin's application was approved by the FIA.

The 1951 race was held under the patronage of the Royal Automobile Club of Spain and for the first time carried the title of Grand Prix of Spain. It attracted one of the most interesting and exciting starting fields of all time: the whole Alfetta stable, several blown and unblown Ferraris, packs of blown Maseratis, and unblown Talbot-Lagos, a single GP OSCA, and a group of tiny, unblown Simca-Gordinis that ran away from everything but the best Alfas and Ferraris.

This was the last race of the season, and the eyes of the whole racing world were on Barcelona since the championship was still in the balance. It was to be the climax in a season-long duel between Ascari and Fangio and between Ferrari and Alfa.

The organizers had expected higher speeds that year and had calculated their lap-speed tables down to 2M 15s, well under Ascari's 2M 24.2s — 94.7 MPH — lap record of the year before. But astonishing technical progress had been made, and Ascari got around in practice in 2M 10.9s — 108.3 MPH. Fangio was almost as quick in best lap time and won the Grand Prix at 98.74 MPH. The entire Spanish-speaking world was euphoric that one of its own had won the world title and, to add to the victory, had won it on the mother country's soil. Alfa Romeo felt that it had proved *its* point and retired permanently from GP racing.

The 1954 race was, of course, for the new 2.5-liter Formula One and it, too, was memorable. It was the first championship appearance of the radically new Lancia GP car. It was the first occasion, after a year of development, on which a Ferrari *Squalo* won a GP. In spite of Pedralbes' extremely fast straightaways, Fangio proved in practice, to everyone's astonishment, that the streamlined, envelope-bodied Mercedes-Benz was slower than the open-wheeled version, which he chose to drive in the race. It was in this race that American Harry Schell turned in one of the finest performances of his career, trimming the 2.5-liter lap record to what was regarded as an amazing 2M 17s. The Mercedes ran poorly, the Lancias, though fast, did not last, and Hawthorn won in a Ferrari. It was a memorable day for the British since this was the second time in history that one of their countrymen had won *two* Grandes Epreuves, the other having been Sir Henry Seagrave, thirty years before. How soon times were to change!

The Pedralbes course was correctly described by its organizers as "one of the most beautiful and spectacular urban circuits in the world." As originally laid out it was 2.77 miles around, was almost perfectly triangular, and its three sides, consisting of immensely wide boulevards, were almost dead straight. Its three corners, though acute (about 34, 50, and 62 degrees), were smooth and wide and allowed plenty of room for

123

driver error. It ran over slightly hilly terrain, and rough stretches of pavement provided a good test of suspension systems.

For the championship races a rectangular 1.13 miles of public streets was added to one side of the triangle, extending its main straight from about 0.7 miles to 1.8 miles. The entire circuit was open to spectators and the big races began at 11 A.M. Thus they were able to end in time for the Spanish midday meal and left the afternoon free for the enjoyment of more basic national diversions such as bullfights and football. International Formula Two racing is still highly popular in Barcelona but there are no plans for the revival of Formula One there at present.

CIRCUIT LENGTH   3.9 miles

RACE DISTANCE   70 laps—273 miles, 1951, 1954

LAP RECORD   105.19 MPH (race). Fangio, Alfa-Romeo Type 159, 1951

ORGANIZERS   Autómovil Club Peña Rhin, 14 Plaza Cataluña, Barcelona, Spain

MONTH   Normally in October

N

AVENIDA DE LA VICTORIA

CARRETERA DE CORNELLA A FOGAS DE TORDERA

PASEO DE MANUEL GIRONA

CALLE DE NUMANCIA

AVENIDA DEL GENERALISIMO FRANCO

START/FINISH

Jarama Circuit

The body and spirit behind motor sport in Spain in recent years has been Jesús Saiz, president of the sports commission of the Royal Spanish Automobile Club in Madrid, the nation's capital. Señor Saiz also is the driving force behind the splendid autodrome about 15 miles from the city, which was completed early in 1967. He is behind the long-range planning leading to this really fascinating new circuit's first Formula One event in 1967 and its first Formula One championship race in 1968.

The autodrome lays claim to being "the most modern in the world." It certainly should rank with the world's best and most interesting. Its concept is the result of collaboration between leading international circuit designer John Hugenholtz, bridge and highway engineer Sandro Rocci, and architects Dominguez Aguado and Rodriguez Riviero. No expense has been spared, and every idea examined in an attempt to profit from all the known successes and failures of the world's road-racing circuits.

Jarama (pronounced Ha*ra*ma) takes its name from a river that winds through this rolling, grassy countryside, which is sprinkled with oaks. It is conveniently situated on the main road between Madrid and Irun.

The autodrome is just one of the permanent installations of the *Club de Jarama*, a "sports city" dedicated to public recreation. It includes three swimming pools, two golf courses, a horseback riding range, a Go-Kart racing track, twenty tennis courts, numerous bars and restaurants, and the road circuit, itself. The terrain on which the circuit is located is ideal for this purpose in every sense and most of the course can be seen at a glance from any point around it.

The strongest emphasis has been placed on driver and spectator safety. For example, the entire track is surrounded by resilient guard rails placed 33 feet back from the pavement's edge. On the outside of each

125

Jarama, near Madrid, is the world's newest Grand Prix circuit. It is clearly one of the finest and one of the most ideally designed.

curve there is a second guard rail, 50 feet back from the first. And on some curves there is yet a third guard rail, 80 feet back from the second. This is admirable.

The course is slightly more than 2 miles long, has 3150 feet of curves and 8200 feet of straights. The longest straight, totally flanked by grandstands, measures 2570 feet; the second-longest measures 1000 feet. There are eleven right-hand curves and six lefts and the total length of the rights is about twice that of the lefts. The radii of the curves range from a hairpin-tight 66 feet to a fast, sweeping 500 feet. Racing is done in the customary clockwise direction.

The Jarama Circuit's lowest point is 2081 feet above sea level and its highest is 2102, making for undulations over an 84-foot vertical range. Exactly one mile of its distance consists of upgrades, the steepest of which is 11.6 percent. There are 1430 feet of downgrade, with a maximum incline of 9 percent.

The cost of creating the track was about $400,000. This and the cost of garages, pits, abundant bleachers, gigantic grandstands and the rest of the permanent structures has been footed entirely by the national club, which is probably the only one in the world to be the owner of its own autodrome. And what is its motive for all this? "Why," says dedicated Señor Saiz, "to restore to Spain her former position in the top league of international motor racing."

CIRCUIT LENGTH   2.131 miles

LAP RECORD   87.17 MPH (race). Clark, Lotus-Ford, 1967 (non-championship)

ORGANIZERS   Comisión Deportiva, Real Automóvil Club de España, General Sanjurjo 10, Madrid, Spain

MONTH   Normally in May

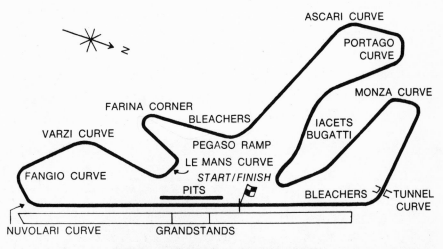

THE SPANISH GRAND PRIX

YEAR	DRIVER	CAR	WINNING SPEED MPH	CIRCUIT
1951	Fangio	Alfa Romeo	98.78	Pedralbes
1954	Hawthorn	Ferrari	97.93	Pedralbes
1968	G. Hill	Lotus-Ford	84.22	Jarama

The Grand Prix of Switzerland

The first Swiss Grand Prix took place in 1934 and, through 1939, (at which point World War II halted all racing) was totally dominated by Mercedes-Benz and Auto Union. It was begun again in 1947, and it became a showplace for Italian superiority until 1953. In 1954 Fangio won the last race there, again for Mercedes. After the Le Mans disaster, religious pressure groups in Switzerland put an end to motor racing in their country.

The Bremgarten Circuit was the cradle and home of Grand Prix racing in Switzerland and was, beyond all argument, one of the finest road-racing courses of all time. Named for the forest through which it wound, on the outskirts of Berne, the 4.5-mile course was very fast, in spite of an almost total lack of any real straights. It was made up mainly of a succession of high-speed bends that put tremendous demands upon

drivers. Naturally, it was one of the classic "driver's circuits." At the same time, it was ideal for spectators. Fans attended in large numbers to witness heroic racing in the misty sunshine and shadow of the great park. The city of Berne loved it all and threw itself into the racing spirit. Streets were draped with racing banners and it was a rare shop window that was not decorated with a racing theme. Everything that happened on the Bremgarten Circuit before the final curtain fell was memorable. The most amazing happening of all was the lap record set in 1936 by Berend Rosemeyer in an Auto Union at 105.4 MPH. No one has ever topped it.

The closest approach to this record was Fangio's 104.48 MPH, turned during practice in 1951 in a Type 159 Alfa Romeo. He also won the race at remarkable speed, considering that it was run in a heavy downpour. The sensation of the 1951 event was Piero Taruffi who, in a 4.5-liter Ferrari, passed Farina's Alfa on the last lap to win second place. Except for his legendary exploits in the *Carrera Panamericana de Mexico*, this was the most brilliant drive of Taruffi's career.

Due to a general lack of suitable Formula One machines the Grandes Epreuves of 1952 and 1953 were contested by cars of the 2-liter Formula

Switzerland. The last Swiss Grand Prix was held on the Bremgarten Circuit at Berne in 1954. Fangio, leading here, was the winner.

Switzerland. The circuit within Bremgarten Park was one of the most beautiful of all, but trees, hay bales, and abruptly changing sunlight and shadow made it dangerous.

Two, which then was in effect. Both first and second places in the 1952 Grand Prix were taken by Ferraris, but the highlight of the occasion was the first appearance on a GP circuit of the radical gull-wing Mercedes-Benz coupés in the *Prix de Berne* for sports cars, which preceded the Grand Prix. One of the four entries was the great Rudy Caracciola, who had won the Swiss GP for Mercedes in 1935, 1937, and 1938. His car went into a high-speed slide, crashed, and Caracciola's left thigh-bone was shattered. He never raced again.

Ascari's Ferrari victory in the 1953 Swiss GP gave him the championship for the second consecutive year. Again in 1954 it was the Swiss GP that decided the championship, this time in favor of Fangio, who lost only two races throughout the season. In his 2.5-liter unsupercharged Mercedes, he turned a practice lap at 104.39 MPH, just a shade under his 1951 practice record in a far more powerful Alfetta.

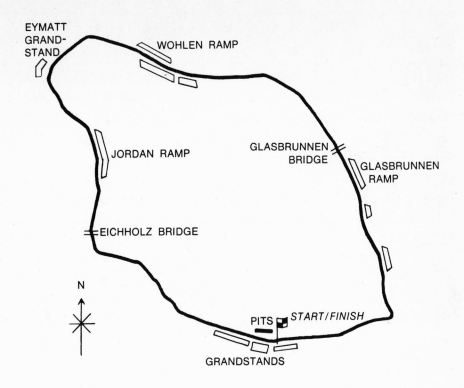

CIRCUIT LENGTH	4.52 miles
RACE DISTANCE	66 laps–298.6 miles, 1954
LAP RECORD	Prewar:
	105.42 MPH (race). Rosemeyer, 6-liter supercharged Auto Union Type C, 1936
	Postwar:
	101.97 MPH (race). Fangio, 2.5-liter Mercedes-Benz Type W196, 1954
ORGANIZERS	Automobile Club der Schweiz, Kochergasse 4, Switzerland
MONTH	Normally in August

131

THE GRAND PRIX OF SWITZERLAND
(Bremgarten Circuit — Berne)

YEAR	DRIVER	CAR	WINNING SPEED MPH
1950	Farina	Alfa Romeo	92.76
1951	Fangio	Alfa Romeo	89.05
1952	Taruffi	Ferrari	92.78–F2
1953	Ascari	Ferrari	97.17–F2
1954	Fangio	Mercedes-Benz	99.17

The Grand Prix of The United States

Indianapolis

By 1908 racing on public roads had been outlawed in nearly every state of the Union. Automobile races on standard oval horse-racing tracks were highly popular throughout the country, and industrialist Carl Fisher conceived the idea of building a huge *paved* track, specifically for automotive use. As originally planned the 2.5-mile oval would merely be the high-speed section of a more intricate circuit, with a road course twisting through its infield, anticipating Monza, Montlhéry, and Brooklands. However, the oval was built first and was such a success that the road-course idea was abandoned. Thus the Speedway Era was born in the United States, and soon there were oval tracks from coast to coast.

Europeans began racing at the Indianapolis Motor Speedway in 1913, and their cars were unbeatable there until 1920, when American cars and drivers became supreme in this specialized type of racing. The year 1927 was the last pre-World War II European entry at Indianapolis, although the 500-mile race continued to be governed by the International formulas established by the AIACR. The Memorial Day event, with its world's richest purse, continued to be listed by the AIACR as one of the Grandes Epreuves.

This tradition carried over into the postwar period even though Americans did not accept the restrictions of FIA Formula One. Therefore, when the drivers' championship was established, points won at Indianapolis counted toward it. Following the 1960 Indianapolis race, the FIA ruled that all championship events must conform to Formula One. But strong forces on both sides of the Atlantic are striving to eliminate the differences between Indianapolis regulations and Formula One and The

133

Speedway may regain its official "classic" status.

The Speedway's two long straights (called "chutes") are each five-eighths of a mile long; the short chutes are one-eighth of a mile, and all four turns are exactly one-quarter of a mile around their center lines. They have a maximum banking of 9 degrees, 12 minutes. The width of the track is 50 feet on the straights and 60 feet on the turns.

In 1966 Scotsman Jim Clark drove his Lotus-Ford to a new lap record of 159.179 MPH. In 1967 American Mario Andretti boosted that record

to an almost incredible 168.982 MPH, driving a Hawk-Ford. The record speed for the 500-mile distance was set in 1967 by American A. J. Foyt at an average of 151.207 MPH. This was Foyt's third Indianapolis victory, and he scored it at the wheel of a Coyote-Ford, a car which he had designed and built.

As so often happens at Indy, the record was good for only one year. In 1968, Bobby Unser won at 152.882 MPH in a Dan Gurney-built Eagle, powered by a turbocharged Offenhauser. Gurney, himself, placed second

135

and Gurney cars ran first, second, and fourth.

It's popular to say that to drive in the "500," all you have to do is "stand on it and turn left." This is untrue. The race is an inferno. It takes very good men to endure it. Any man who wins it is a pretty good driver.

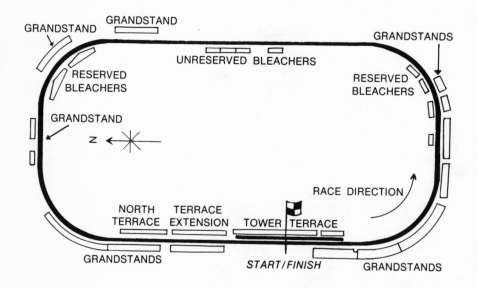

Sebring

The first FIA Formula-One Grand Prix of the United States took place at Sebring, Florida, in December, 1959. The event had first been scheduled by the FIA for a date in March, but conflicts arose and the new date was assigned, following the next-to-last championship race of the year by a full three months. No one could have known at the time that this would be the salvation of the United States GP, getting the series off to a historic start, and preventing a fiasco. Among the beneficiaries of this sequence of events were the international sport, the sport in the United States, and Alec Ulmann.

Alec Ulmann was educated on both sides of the Atlantic, occupies himself with the aircraft industry on both sides of the Atlantic, and therefore thinks in very international terms. He has loved cars and racing since early childhood and, when road racing revived in the United States just after World War II, it was his enthusiasm that created "America's Little Le Mans": the Sebring 12 Hour Race for sports cars. The location was ghastly — a million miles from nowhere, midway between Tampa and Miami in the sandy brush country of central Florida.

The racing plant itself suited local conditions. It was laid out on a vast abandoned air field. *Autocar* described it as "what must be the flattest and most featureless aerodrome ever used for motor racing . . . dull, both for spectators and drivers. It is not, by any stretch of the imagination, a grand prix circuit." But it was a place to go road racing in a country that knew almost nothing about road racing. Ulmann had found the unlikely spot with the help of Sam and Miles Collier and by his own vision and dynamic enterprise he turned it into the sports-car racing capital of the hemisphere. His goal was to bring Formula One Grand Prix racing to the United States.

Ulmann's twelve-hour classics at Sebring achieved the highest inter-

137

national status, so that when he applied for a place on the Grand Prix calendar he did so as one of the world's foremost race organizers and his request was granted automatically. It was up to him to provide the incentive to attract the racing teams.

The usual incentive is money and its usual source is vast crowds of paying spectators. Getting them to the boondocks of Florida to witness the first-ever Formula One race on American soil was a gamble calculated to attract few fans. And then, at the start of the season, the date was delayed, placing the United States GP at the very tail end of the

season. It also placed Ulmann in the driver's seat as far as the competition year was concerned. This was because the GP of Italy had failed to decide the championship.

It was still within the grasp of Moss (Cooper), Brabham (Cooper), or Brooks (Ferrari), and therefore the show absolutely had to go on. It was ironic that the constructors involved had no choice but to ship their cars and crews thousands of miles to a new race in the New World in order to resolve a contest that still was essentially European. Ulmann did a magnificent job of preparing his circuit for a Grande Epreuve. Money was something else again, and the total purse amounted to $15,750, plus the bounty of a quarter of an acre of raw homesite in nearby Orange Blossom Lakeside Estates for the winner.

The cars and the talent came, not because they wanted to but because they had to. The crowd, such as it was, consisted mainly of hard-core road-racing enthusiasts who knew enough and cared enough to make the pilgrimage into the wilderness and to sacrifice themselves to the naked avarice of local landlords. Spectators had their reward in the form of one of the most dramatic races in history.

Few of them ever had seen a Formula One car in action. Many of them had been there in 1958 and had watched Moss prune the lap record to a blistering 3M 20s in an Aston-Martin. This time, during the first day of practice, they witnessed the same driver chop the lap record to a really astonishing three minutes, flat.

In the race Moss, driving a Cooper-Climax, led comfortably until gearbox failure put him out on the fifth lap, again eliminating his championship hopes. Brabham flew into the lead as Ferraris fell like flies around him. Then, only a mile from the finish, a leaking line caused him to run out of fuel. He coasted for half a mile before the public-address system announced that his Cooper had stopped. As Brabham's teammate, Bruce McLaren, flew by in a sister car to score his first GP win, Moss hiked up the course to cheer Brabham on. The Australian pushed his car the rest of the distance, crossed the finish line in fourth place, and collapsed from exhaustion. But the championship was his.

Sebring's 5.2-mile course has four curves, five corners, two hairpin turns, and a zigzag. About two-thirds of its surface consists of concrete runways that become extremely slippery when wet, which was not the case for the United States GP there. The remaining third consists of as-phalt-surfaced former access roads. The longest straight measures 4,700 feet and two others of 3,900 and 3,600 make this a very rapid track.

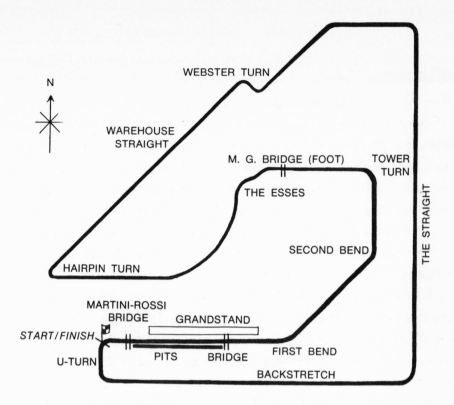

CIRCUIT LENGTH	5.2 miles
RACE DISTANCE	42 laps–218.4 miles, 1959
LAP RECORD	101.18 MPH (race). Trintignant, 2.5-liter Cooper-Climax, 1959
ORGANIZERS	Automobile Racing Club of Florida, Sebring, Florida, U.S.A.
MONTH	Normally in December

Riverside

It is very likely that automobile-racing enthusiasm is not stronger any-where on earth than in Southern California. Postwar road racing developed quickly there on whatever courses could be found or scrounged and, from early in the 1950's, there were constant rumors that magnificent road-racing circuits were about to be built. They came to nothing until Los Angeles restaurateur and Mercedes-Benz 300SL pilot Rudy Cleye bought 528 acres of rolling desert, about 5 miles south of the town of Riverside and 60 miles south of America's western metropolis, Los Angeles.

What Cleye had visualized for Riverside would cost $800,000 before the first bleachers were up, and this spelled strain. Then he was rescued by older, wiser, equally fanatic, and much wealthier John Edgar, a patron of the sport in the very grand manner. In late 1957, Riverside International Raceway was established.

The setting is magnificent: clean, bare desert backed by majestic, towering mountains and open to the setting sun. In its general character it has much in common with Zandvoort and Casablanca but it is unique. Part of the course is very close to being a hill-climb, while the rest is fast and level. Among the ideal racing circuits it is one of the best by almost every criterion: safety, visibility, easy access and exit, and excellent driving challenge. It needs better grandstands and permanent structures and it must suffer eternally from the local winds and from the tons of dust and sand which they move from A to B, B being the track, yourself, and your car.

After having presented the United States with its first Grand Prix, Alec Ulmann lost no time in realizing that Sebring was not the ideal spot. Riverside could be that spot and he secured its use for the second United States GP. Ulmann did a magnificent job of organization and

U.S.A. — Riverside. The 1960 United States GP was held on Southern California's excellent Riverside Raceway and was won by Stirling Moss.

was rewarded with another stellar entry field of Europeans who were more than willing to race for nothing, if necessary, in order to cultivate a potentially rich new market for their wares. Ulmann made just one mistake: he expected to be received hospitably in Southern California.

Publishers of major newspapers in Southern California had decided there was important money to be made through the sponsorship of road racing, above all on the outstanding Riverside Circuit. Mr. Ulmann was under the impression that his historic event was newsworthy but the newspapers decided that it was not, and it took place without news coverage. In spite of this a hard-core crowd of perhaps 15,000 turned out for this important racing contest on American soil, one of the last of the Grandes Epreuves of the 2.5-liter formula, which had been in effect for seven thrilling years.

Those who were competent to judge heaved a sigh of relief over the choice of the new circuit, as opposed to what they had seen at Sebring the year before. They liked its nine bends and corners, its esses, its long straights, its very fast and sweeping final curve, and its abundant safety features. Drivers were enthusiastic, which they had not been at Sebring.

Moss dominated practice, during which he guided his Lotus to a masterful new lap record of 1M 54.4s. He also dominated and won the race. Brabham, in a Cooper, turned the fastest lap during the race in 1M 56.3s, but a series of engine-compartment fires held him back to a fourth-place finish. Nevertheless, he won the championship for the second year in a row.

The history of the United States GP might have been very different if Alec Ulmann had had substantial funds with which to promote the Riverside event in Southern California's major communications media. Since he did not, the unaware public stayed away and it fell to others to keep United States GP racing alive.

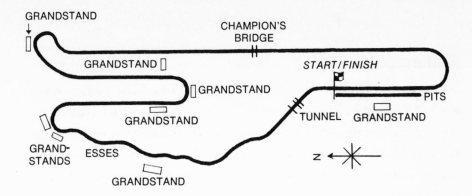

CIRCUIT LENGTH	3.273 miles
RACE DISTANCE	75 laps–245.63 miles, 1960
LAP RECORD	100.9 MPH (race). Brabham, 2.5-liter Cooper-Climax, 1960
ORGANIZERS	Riverside International Raceway, Riverside, California
MONTH	Normally in November

Watkins Glen

The Sports Car Club of America (SCCA) had about 150 members when, at a gathering at Indianapolis in May, 1948, Cameron and Jean Argetsinger expressed their desire for a road-racing circuit in upper New York State. It would run through and around the town of Watkins Glen. Cameron and his wife had already charted the public roads that could be converted into a 6.6-mile circuit.

Although road racing had been dead in the United States for decades the SCCA's membership cheered this proposal. A month later Alec Ulmann motored into the quiet village of Watkins Glen at the wheel of an ancient and magnificent 4.5-liter Bentley. This founding father of the modern sport in America was empowered to deal with the local authorities on behalf of the SCCA. Amazingly enough, here, too, everyone liked the idea, from town Mayor Erway to the Department of Public Works in the state capital.

And so the first Watkins Glen Grand Prix for sports cars was held on October 2, 1948. It was the first of a continuing series of colossal successes that were to have the most profound influence on the development of automotive sport and enthusiasm in the United States.

In 1949 an estimated 100,000 spectators were on hand to prove that road racing could have a brilliant future here. In 1950 the Watkins Glen GP was honored with inclusion on the FIA International Calendar. The following year was another of great progress and achievement and 1952 promised to be the same. Then, during the race, spectators pushed too close to the outside of the curve at Old Corning Hill. A car brushed them, injuring seven and killing a child. That was the end of the old circuit.

But the race had been very good for the community, and its Chamber of Commerce quickly attended to the creation of the Watkins Glen Grand

146

U.S.A. — Watkins Glen. Since 1961 Watkins Glen, in upstate New York, has been the home of the United States GP. The lack of crowd control, shown here, is lamentable.

Prix Corporation, with Argetsinger as its head. Another, safer course was laid out and the GP took place on schedule on September 18, 1953. But the real, long-term answer was a tailormade road circuit on private ground. The corporation forged ahead with such a plan.

The land was located and a superb course was designed, with the collaboration of Bill Milliken and other scientists of the Aeronautical Laboratory of Cornell University. A bond issue was floated to cover the heavy construction costs and the townspeople of the Glen itself were the major and most eager investors. The new circuit was inaugurated on September 15, 1956, and the success story went on.

After the unfortunate financial failure of the first two Formula One Grands Prix of the United States the future of the event was grim. But Watkins Glen already had a long history of making racing support itself and confidently applied to the FIA for authorization to conduct the Third United States GP. Arrangement of the details took time, so that the actual starting field remained unknown until practice began, two days before the event. Everyone came but Ferrari, which meant BRM, Cooper, and

U.S.A. — Watkins Glen. Because of its highly varied circuit and beautiful rustic setting, this autumn race is one of the most popular on the international calendar.

Lotus. Sixty thousand spectators saw Innes Ireland (Lotus) score his first championship win at an average of 103.22 MPH. No one got close to Moss's 1960 lap record during a Formula Libre (no limit) race at the Glen of 109.24 MPH, at the wheel of a 2.5-liter Lotus.

Watkins Glen is as agreeable to drivers as it is to spectators. The race is always held in autumn, when the leaves have begun to blaze with color and the whole charming, rustic countryside is bathed in natural beauty. The 2.3-mile circuit is located about 5 miles southeast of the town. It climbs and weaves through alternately wooded and open terrain and gives the deceptive impression of being a slow circuit, which it certainly is not. Since it is located in the heart of a popular tourist area, good accommodations are abundant, including camping and trailer facilities at the track. Practice sessions are generously long and there are two large garage buildings at the circuit, which the teams share and where they can be observed at work. They tend to stay and gather at the Glen Motor Lodge, about ten minutes' drive from the course.

Beginning with and ever since its first United States GP Watkins Glen has done a superlative job of conducting this event and of lifting it to major international status.

In 1966 Jim Clark gave the H16 BRM its first-ever victory when he drove his Lotus to an average of 114.94 MPH for 248.4 miles in the Eighth United States GP. In 1967 Jim Clark was victorious here again, this time driving a Lotus-Ford.

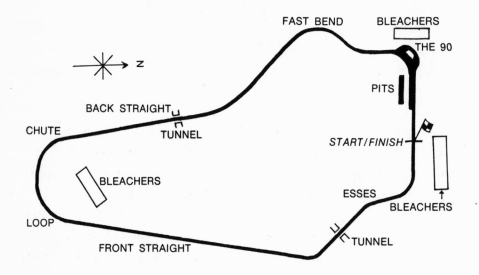

CIRCUIT LENGTH	2.3 miles
RACE DISTANCE	108 laps–248.4 miles
LAP RECORD	124.45 MPH (race). G. Hill, Lotus-Ford, 1967
ORGANIZERS	Watkins Glen Grand Prix Corporation, Watkins Glen, N.Y.
MONTH	Normally in September/October

150

THE GRAND PRIX OF THE UNITED STATES

YEAR	DRIVER	CAR	WINNING SPEED MPH	CIRCUIT
1959	McLaren	Cooper	98.83	Sebring
1960	Moss	Lotus	99.00	Riverside
1961	Ireland	Lotus	103.17	Watkins Glen
1962	Clark	Lotus	108.61	Watkins Glen
1963	G. Hill	BRM	108.91	Watkins Glen
1964	G. Hill	BRM	111.10	Watkins Glen
1965	G. Hill	BRM	107.98	Watkins Glen
1966	Clark	Lotus	114.94	Watkins Glen
1967	Clark	Lotus-Ford	120.95	Watkins Glen

The One-of-a-Kind Grands Prix

The Grand Prix of Pescara

Pescara, Italy, is a fine example of the subtle currents that can play between earth-shaking world affairs and Grand Prix racing. Why was there a Formula One race in 1957 at this outpost of civilization that counted toward the drivers' championship?

Well, there was the usual Italian lament: "Why must we poor Italians have just a single big race, and no more than anybody else?" But that was an old story.

The new story was that in the previous November the French had hurled themselves into what proved to be a disastrous attack upon Egypt. The Suez Canal was closed, Europe was freezing for lack of stove oil, and it appeared that the Grands Prix of France and Britain would be canceled because of the shortage of appropriate petroleum products. At that time there were no Grands Prix in the United States, Mexico, or South Africa, and it seemed pointless to conduct a World Championship for Drivers on the basis of the smattering of races which could be counted on to take place. Hence, Pescara.

Giving Italy two Grandes Epreuves was criticized, but no one could complain about the superb 16-mile, coast-to-mountain-summit minor edition of the Targa Florio. The first race over this long, bone-crushing course had been won by Enzo Ferrari in 1924, at the wheel of an Alfa Romeo. Now it was to be contested by Coopers, Maseratis, three Vanwalls, and a single Ferrari. Moss won the hard-fought race, with Fangio's Maserati hard on his tail.

152

Pescara. American Masten Gregory (Maserati) winds through the town section of the 16-mile hill-and-dale circuit.

Grand Prix Championship Courses and Drivers

CIRCUIT LENGTH	16 miles
RACE DISTANCE	18 laps—289 miles
LAP RECORD	97.87 MPH (race). Moss, Vanwall
WINNER	Moss, Vanwall, 95.82 MPH
ORGANIZERS	Automobile Club di Pescara, Pescara, Italy
MONTH	Normally in August

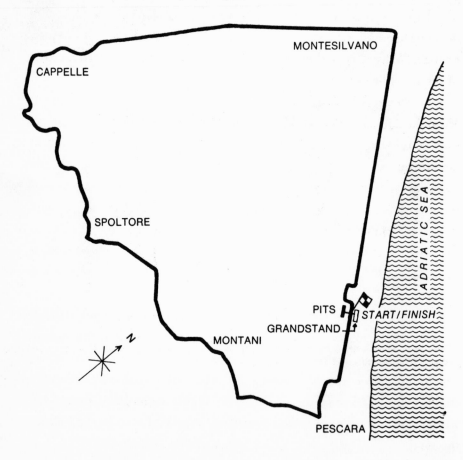

The Grand Prix of Morocco

The first Casablanca Grand Prix took place on the Anfa Circuit in 1931 and the last in 1934; it seems to have been an outing for Frenchmen which lost its allure with the appearance of the big German cars.

During the 1950's sports-car racing became popular here; and in 1957, with the pressures of Suez threatening racing in Europe, Casablanca's racing entrepreneur leaped into the breach by organizing a Formula One race. It had the blessing of Morocco's King Mohammed V, who happens to be an all-out automotive enthusiast. Among the more than one hundred cars in the royal garage today are several Rolls-Royces, Ferraris, Maseratis, and ten Checker airport limousines for the transport of the royal harem.

With the green light from His Majesty, the Royal Automobile Club of Morocco accomplished wonders in which any European or American club could take pride. The small sports-car circuit was their point of departure, but it was to form only part of the Grand Prix track. Six weeks before the big race it was unfinished and the grandstands, timers' stand, and press box did not exist. In that short period the entire installation was completed, including permanent structures, good, solid parking areas on top of the sand, and a paved course of the first quality. It was called the Ain Diab Circuit, for the suburb of Casablanca in which it lies.

The desert setting is quite beautiful. The main straight runs parallel with the sea, actually within a stone's throw of the breakers that roll in from the Atlantic. There are only two slow curves on the 4.7-mile course, which describes a roughly rectangular, undulating path over the palm-studded dunes. Most of the drivers were highly enthusiastic over it but with one universal reservation: something would have to be done about the sand.

155

Morocco. Stirling Moss (Vanwall) leads Phil Hill to win the Moroccan Grand Prix held on the Ain Diab Circuit in 1958.

The first Moroccan Grand Prix was held under royal patronage and the drivers and other personages of the occasion were guests of the monarch in the palace at Rabat. The race was won by Behra (Maserati) at 112.64 MPH, followed by Lewis-Evans (Vanwall) and Trintignant (BRM). Thus the event qualified for the drivers' championship of the following year.

The eyes of the racing world were on Ain Diab at the end of 1958. It was the last of ten championship races and still the title was undecided, a toss-up between Moss (Vanwall) and Hawthorn (Ferrari).

Our old friend and showman Toto Roche was the official starter, and when the flag fell Moss shot into the lead, with Phil Hill (Ferrari) right on his tail. Hill was not in the championship's upper bracket that year but this did not keep him from driving to win. Hill got ahead. Then Moss swept by him on the inside of a bend and forced Hill down the escape road in what one British journal described as "a pretty display of track-craft."

Hill hustled back into the fray but had lost an irreplaceable half minute. Ten laps before the finish of the 55-lap event Hill still was in second place, pursuing Moss. Then came the signal from the Ferrari pits and Phil lifted, letting Hawthorn go by. The race ended with the first three drivers in that order. His second place gave Hawthorn 42 points and the championship, versus Moss's 41.

In October Morocco was a welcome relief from the wintry north, and a popular race while it lasted. But it was the creation of one man and he was killed in a highway accident the following year.

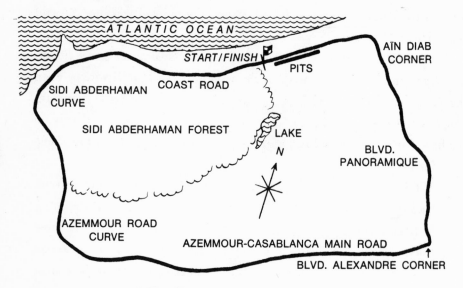

CIRCUIT LENGTH	4.73 miles
RACE DISTANCE	55 laps–260 miles
LAP RECORD	119.6 MPH (race). Moss, Vanwall
WINNER	Moss, Vanwall, 116.22 MPH
ORGANIZERS	Royal Automobile Club of Morocco, Place des Nations-Unies, Casablanca, Morocco
MONTH	Normally in October

Zeltweg — The Grand Prix of Austria

I have not had the luck to attend a GP at Zeltweg but Martin Lewis of *Autocar* was there in 1966 and describes it as, "The funniest GP race I've ever seen." Spectator facilities were nil, the press stand consisted of four rows of planks, the marshaling of the race was a travesty, and the timers' stand was a broken-down London bus which had been months in getting to Austria because it constantly jammed its roof under low-clearance bridges and overpasses. It still carried the painted warning, "Avoid Rush Hour Travel."

This was hardly necessary since Zeltweg is locked away in the Steiermark province of Austria high in the valley of the Mur River, between the pine-clad Seckauer Tauren and the Glenialpe, these being mountain ranges. Zeltweg was once the site of a NATO fighter base; and it is on the base's still highly operational runways that sports-car races have been held for several years.

In 1963 the inspiration arose locally to organize a Formula One event, and it was won by Jack Brabham (Brabham-Climax) at 96.34 MPH. A crowd of about 80,000 was present for the occasion, plus a force of three policemen. During the final laps of the race the course took on the aspect of New Year's Eve at Times Square and the horrified clerk of the course — Schmitz of Germany — stopped the impending carnage with two laps to go.

Having staged its first Formula One Grand Prix Zeltweg applied for championship status for 1964. The CSI observers who had been present required many improvements, among the most important of which was the repair of the track's surface. It was so rough that it had reduced many fine cars to scrap. Everything was promised, and Zeltweg became the sixth in 1964's ten championship events.

The stellar field arrived and found the hockey-stick-shaped course in

the same condition. There was still the choppy surface, the tar strips sticking up between the concrete slabs, and the drainage gutter that ran straight across the fastest bend on the circuit. But the show had to go on and practice began, accompanied by daredevil aerobatics of a squadron of Austrian SAAB-Draken fighter planes overhead.

In the presence of Princess Irena and Prince Carlos, twenty good cars took the starting flag. At about half-distance in the 105-lap event, the gearbox of Phil Hill's Cooper locked up and the car flipped and crashed, throwing Hill onto the track. He was uninjured and busied himself by trying to get to the fire extinguisher of his car, which was slowly burning.

As the course marshals stood and watched and a fire truck made its leisurely approach, the Cooper's fuel tank exploded. Fortunately, Hill was out of the car; and had he been in it, no one would have been around to help.

This Austrian GP was won by Bandini (Ferrari) at 99.20 MPH. He was followed by Ginther (BRM), and Bob Anderson (Brabham). The other seventeen cars had been reduced to assorted states of wreckage.

A real road circuit has been projected for Zeltweg and there is talk of its being opened in 1968. It will take more than that to bring back the embittered Formula One contestants.

Grand Prix Championship Courses and Drivers

CIRCUIT LENGTH	1.98 miles
RACE DISTANCE	105 laps–208.7 miles
LAP RECORD	101.5 MPH (race). Gurney, Brabham-Climax
WINNER	Bandini, Ferrari, 99.20 MPH
ORGANIZERS	Österreichischer Automobil-Montorrad und Touring Club, Schubertring 9, Vienna 1, Austria
MONTH	Normally in August

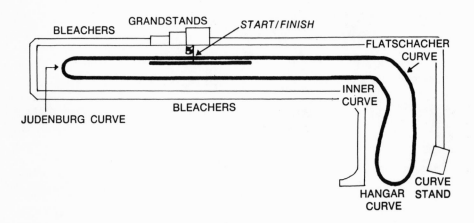

II

The Champions

Nino Farina

The first man to win the World Championship of Drivers was Dr. Giuseppe Antonio Farina. He was born in Turin, Italy, on October 30, 1906 — the very day that his father, Giovanni, founded the famous coach-building firm of Stabilimenti Farina. He was named for one of his father's brothers who was best known as *Pinin* — the local diminutive for Giuseppe. This uncle, when world famous in his own right, became bored with being taken for his celebrated nephew every time he was introduced and had his name legally changed to Pininfarina, thereby founding a new dynasty.

The nephew distinguished himself from his uncle by going under the diminutive for Antonio, Nino. Having been born into a great automotive family, he acquired a passion for cars as soon as he left the cradle. To this love for fine machines he added a love for fine horses and did his military service in the Italian Cavalry. A highly intelligent youth, he was trained to inherit the management of his father's firm and he earned a Doctor of Law degree at the University of Turin.

The whole family had an avid appetite for racing, and Nino rode in his first automotive contest at the age of seventeen as copilot with Pinin in the Aosta-Great St. Bernard "hill-climb" — actually a flat-out race up the side of the Alps. Then his father bought a pair of 1500 cc Alfas so that they could share this sport together. In the same mountain race in 1928 Nino crashed and broke his collar bone. His father disposed of the fine little sports cars.

In 1933 no one could restrain Nino from his passion; he bought a 2.3 Alfa and began winning races. He showed enough brilliance to have it recognized by Ernesto Maserati early in 1934, and this great driver-engineer put Nino at the wheel of one of his 1500 cc *monoposti*, which

Giuseppe (Nino) Farina was known as "The Stylist" for his serene, poised driving form. Here he drives a Type 158 Alfa-Romeo at Monza in 1947.

enabled him to go Grand Prix racing on the international level. This threw him into direct competition with many of the greatest drivers of all time; among them were Caracciola, Chiron, Varzi, and Nuvolari. He was a star student in a most remarkable school and from Varzi he absorbed an imperturbable calm while, from Nuvolari, he learned his famous straight-arm driving attitude. To this he added his own cavalry officer's erect-in-the-saddle posture, and it was not long before Nino was known as "The Stylist." His superb, smooth style was a major influence on the generation of drivers that appeared after the war, two of the best examples being Fangio and Moss.

Farina was young in 1934 and his great teachers were not. In spite of German domination of Grand Prix racing he went from success to success, and in 1935 he was plucked by Enzo Ferrari to become a member of the Alfa Romeo team.

As such, he finished second in the *Mille Miglia* 1,000-miles in 1936 and again in 1937. He took part in almost innumerable races, always placing among the foremost as long as his luck held out. In 1936 he was trailing Nuvolari, the winner of the American Vanderbilt Cup Race, when his steering broke. In 1937 he finished fifth in the same event.

He earned enough victories and points to win the Italian championship title in 1936, then again in 1937. In 1938 Nuvolari went over to the German Auto Union team. Nino became Alfa's Number One driver and won his national championship for the third time. In 1940 he won the last of the prewar Grandes Epreuves, the Grand Prix of Tripoli. He was at the very peak of his form when his career was interrupted by World War II. He had to pass the war years as an officer in the Italian Armored Cavalry.

As soon as the war was over Farina was back in racing and he won one of the first postwar Grands Prix at Geneva in 1946. In 1948 he won the Mar del Plata Grand Prix in Argentina, along with the Grands Prix of Geneva and Monaco, driving Maseratis and Ferraris.

In 1950 he returned to the Alfa team and his victories were overwhelming. He won the Italian championship for the fourth time and the championship of the world for the first time in history. In 1951 his wins continued and he became champion of Italy for the fifth time. He was still a magnificent driver in 1955, when, at the age of forty-nine and heavily scarred and battered, he retired from racing.

Farina had a reputation for being nerveless, callous, and heartless. He was involved in a multitude of accidents, many of which came close to taking his life and several of which took the lives of spectators and other drivers. He was grateful to the staff of *Road & Track Magazine* for the gift of a crash helmet that saved his life in a Turin Grand Prix, but otherwise he was unmoved by these events. He lived by the adage that to make an omelette you have to break a few eggs. He was proud, jealous, arrogant, and a problem member of any team. He was convinced of his superiority and made no secret of his resentment of stellar team-members such as Wimille and Fangio. Rodney Walkerly wrote in *The Motor* (London):

Farina was icy calm, grimly determined and quite ruthless. No one

Farina was working in the MGM film Grand Prix *when he was killed in a road accident in 1966, a few days after this photo was taken.*

attempted to struggle with him for a corner. His face was impassive in triumph or defeat.

I saw the battle-scarred veteran during practice for the 1966 Monaco Grand Prix. He was driving one of the race cars in the MGM film-in-progress, *Grand Prix*. Not many members of the youthful crowd knew who this giant was, but he still knew. He obviously reveled at being back in the saddle, exuded all his old force, and was spiritedly conversational. I asked him why he had not written the story of his most remarkable career.

"I don't even want to remember it," he said. "There are too many rotten tales. There was too much heartbreak. If you want a book to write you should listen to my wife's story. Call it *The Wife of a Champion*. What our women endure has never been told, and it should be."

Five weeks later Nino Farina put his Lotus Cortina — according to the local police — into a curve in the French Alps just a bit too fast. It was his last accident.

167

Juan Manuel Fangio

1951, 1954, 1955, 1956, 1957

I once had the unforgettable experience of being Fangio's interpreter and guide for five solid days. Our trails have crossed many times since but always under conditions of pressure. On that occasion we just shopped for race cars, witnessed engine tests, and talked.

Fangio was on his way to Indianapolis to survey the track. The "500" was the last major racing challenge that he had not mastered and he had a strong desire to win it. He was, as always, utterly frank.

"You Americans say it's a simple race. I don't think so. I won't tackle it until I've studied the course and am convinced that I can do well on it, which I'm not at all sure of right now. As the Champion of the World one should not do poorly. One owes it to that honor to perform in a manner befitting it. It is a heavy burden."

He felt the same way, necessarily, about the car he wanted to buy. It had to be a sure-fire top contender. American rules still permitted 3 liters supercharged versus 4.5 liters unblown. This, he knew, gave a huge advantage to the supercharged engine, provided it was reliable. It failed to prove so and Fangio decided to pass up Indianapolis rather than be an also-ran. It is not that he was an egotist or a bad sportsman; it was his sense of responsibility. He felt it primarily, I know, toward his countrymen, but he also felt it very strongly toward the racing public throughout the world. He was not a showman; he was a professional's professional, dedicated body and soul to his calling.

In 1948, when he began his career as Argentina's greatest unofficial ambassador, his country was scarcely known to the world. Juan Manuel, born there on June 24, 1911, enjoyed a smattering of schooling until he was ten, when he went to work in a squalid machine shop. He and his

Juan Manuel Fangio at the height of his glory. Most authorities rank him as the greatest driver of all time.

whole little town of Balcarce spent their lives with tightened belts; and to work like a man while he was still a child was normal. In 1929, at the age of eighteen, he took his first racing ride in a battered, hopped-up Chevvy.

In 1935 he could afford to build his own single-seat Ford V8 road-racing machine. In it and other cars he became a fixture of the Argentine racing scene, driving on dirt tracks, paved oval tracks, on park circuits, in road races, and finally in the incredible, continent-spanning modified stock-car races that still are a feature of the sport in South America. By 1948 he was one of a handful of superior drivers in a nation for which automobile racing is a major national sport.

General Juan Domingo Perón had made the federal support of popular sport an important part of his "New Argentina" program. He was passionately fond of cars and car racing and, through the Automobile Club of Argentina, launched a plan for the encouragement and development of native racing talent. It produced some great drivers, including the greatest of them all: Fangio.

Up to that time practically all automobile racing in Argentina was done with modified stock cars. Perón encouraged Grand Prix racing by importing talent and cars from Europe, and his government invested in a few GP cars for the club to use as training vehicles for promising pilots. Fangio was given his first ride in a GP car early in 1948. He sat in the little supercharged Maserati for a moment, studying the controls.

169

Then he blasted off and, after a couple of practice laps, lapped the circuit within a second of its record. It was instantly apparent that Fangio and GP cars were made for each other.

Perón sent him to Europe that year, "just to study and observe." He reconnoitered the major international circuits. He got a ride in a 1.5-liter supercharged Gordini in the French GP at Reims and clocked the fastest lap before the car's fuel tank split. That was his start in big-time road racing.

The following year trail-blazer Fangio was sent back to Europe at the head of a group of promising drivers, including Froilán Gonzales. The great Italian driver, Varzi, had helped to train them in Argentina and they named their team for him. During this first European racing season Fangio (Maserati) won his first event, the GP of San Remo. He started in nine races that year and won six. In 1950 he drove for Alfa Romeo, winning three of the six championship events. Farina nosed him out of the title by three points but for Fangio the FIA created the title of sub-champion.

In 1951 Fangio continued with Alfa, won the Swiss and the French GP's, took second in the British and German and clinched the championship by winning the Spanish. He made a pilgrimage to Varzi's grave, near Milan, to give silent thanks to his friend and teacher. The reception that greeted the conquering hero in Argentina was beyond all description.

Alfa withdrew from racing, and in 1952 Fangio drove for BRM. The brilliant cars did not run well and for Fangio every failure was like a betrayal of friends and loved ones at home.

His luck improved in 1953, with Maserati. His win in the Italian and seconds in the French, British, and German GP's placed him second in the championship once more.

In 1954 he won the Argentine and Belgian GP's for Maserati and then, driving for Mercedes-Benz, he won the French, German, Swiss, and

Italian GP's. He also won the championship by a margin of 17 points. In 1955, still with Mercedes, he won it again by an identical, huge margin. He placed first in the Argentine, Belgian, Dutch, and Italian, and second in the British GP.

In 1956 he drove Lancia-Ferraris, winning the Argentine, British, and German GP's and finishing second at Monaco and Monza. He won the championship from Moss by 3 points. Since one of his first and two of his second places were shared with co-drivers, Moss would have won the championship under the later-revised scoring system.

In 1957 Fangio won the Argentine, Monaco, French, and German GP's and was second at Monza and Pescara, which gave him his fifth championship by a 15-point margin. Then after the French GP at Reims, where he had started twenty years before, he retired. He was still at the peak of his greatness, but at forty-seven and after two hundred races and seventy-eight victories he admitted that he was beginning to feel his age.

It is impossible in this short space to begin to do any justice to Fangio, a phenomenal human being. Not that he is complex — he is the opposite. He is quiet, modest, shy, and a gentleman even under fierce racing conditions. He is short, huskily built, has light-brown hair, pale-blue eyes and, like Caracciola, a surprisingly high-pitched voice. From the start of his GP career he was terribly fast and somewhat reckless. By 1950 he was terribly fast and smooth, in the manner of his idol, Varzi. In his day his stamina was unequaled, his reactions like the speed of light, and his judgment — particularly in moments of crisis — exquisite. While Moss is one of the most restless men I have ever known, Fangio is one of the most relaxed. He can and does sleep anywhere and at any time. He was wonderfully gentle to cars, while wringing their utmost from them.

He was and is deeply loyal. When Ferrari chose to attack him he let it pass. When "Dictator" Perón fell from grace Fangio did not cease to give grateful credit to the man who had done so much to make his career possible. At the same time, Fangio always has lived entirely aloof from politics.

He is a very intelligent person with a Buddha-like serenity. Long before his retirement he began to provide carefully for his parents' future, his family's, and his own. He is a *very* important personage in the Argentine business world today. Along with the immortal singer, Carlos Gardel, he is one of his country's greatest popular heroes. He still serves his country in the best way he knows, by training new Argentine racing drivers. He is doing his best to produce a new Fangio, which is impossible.

On one of the many occasions when Stirling Moss has been asked if it was not crushing to him never to have won the championship, he said, "Not at all. If I were to win it six times it wouldn't make me better than Fangi . . . because I'm not. I don't think anyone will ever match Fangio. He is the greatest driver that ever lived."

Alberto Ascari

1952, 1953

It is very rare for a son to match the achievements of a great father and even more rare when he excels them.

Alberto "Ciccio" Ascari was born in Milan on July 13, 1918. His father, Antonio, operated a commercial garage, began racing cars in 1911, and was one of the world's finest drivers when the Alfa Romeo P2 GP car made its debut in 1924. He was signed as a team driver and the papers were calling him "champion of champions" when he was killed on July 26, 1925. He was far in the lead of the French GP at Montlhery and was thirty-six years old.

Shortly after the accident his teammate, the equally great Giuseppe Campari, visited the widow, Elisa, and her two children. Alberto was only seven but he never forgot how the burly giant picked him up, held him in his arms, and said, "Someday you will arrive at the heights as he did. Perhaps you will be even more famous." He kissed the boy on both cheeks and brusquely left.

Alberto was not an easy child for Elisa to raise. When he was eleven, he said to his mother at the end of his school term, "*Basta* with all this talking about other people. Now I want others to talk about me."

Racing was the one road to fame he understood and admired. Still only eleven, he found a friend who would lend him a motorcycle. He began racing and doing quite well. He began staying away from school and when his mother would scold him he would say, "I don't want to study and I don't want to work. I want to race motorcycles."

By 1936 he had squeezed enough out of his small allowance and poker earnings to buy his own 500 cc bike. That was the end of his schooling and he went racing full time. He was so good that in 1937 he became a

173

In the blood. Alberto Ascari's father, Antonio, was one of Italy's greatest champions.

member of the Bianchi factory team, with which he became a consistent top finisher.

By 1939 he had won enough in prize money to invest in a small Fiat agency and to turn his thoughts to racing cars. It was at this period that he met brilliant driver Gigi Villoresi.

Young Ascari's personality was pure sunshine. In addition to being modest, warm, friendly, cheerful, and always smiling, he also had an exuberant, off-beat sense of humor. The pudgy Ascari was no more afflicted with the stiff decorum of Northern Italy than the lean, aristocratic Villoresi. They fell into immediate, profound friendship and their antics lent color to the sport for years.

Villoresi passed on all his considerable driving knowledge to the younger man, emphasizing the primary importance of careful study of racing circuits and machinery. He got Ascari his first racing ride on four wheels in an early Fiat-engined Ferrari in the 1940 *Mille Miglia*. It was he who sold Ascari his first one-man racing car that year — a super-charged, eight-cylinder Maserati. And it was he who, in 1949, was instrumental in getting Ascari onto the Ferrari team.

After he had driven only three races in 1940 the war began. He returned to competition in March of 1947 and won his first victory that year in the *Circuito di Modena*. In 1948, still driving his own Maserati,

174

he participated in eleven important races, which included two outright wins and a second place at Silverstone. He began the 1949 season with the General Perón GP in Buenos Aires, in his Maserati. Then Ferrari signed him on; he had excellent cars to drive and was on his way. That year he drove in another eleven races but this time won the Grands Prix of Bari, Switzerland, France, Britain, Europe, and, again, the Perón. This was the formal beginning that led to his championship in 1952 and 1953.

Ascari was a fearless charger. While driving a much faster car, I had the opportunity to follow, for several mountainous miles, the Detroit sedan in which he practiced for the 1952 Mexican Road Race. The highway was open to normal traffic, yet he took blind turns on the wrong side of the road as though he were indestructable. With almost 2000 miles to go he destroyed his Ferrari within 25 miles of the start.

He made his debut in England on the crest of the wave of motor-racing enthusiasm that was building there. His skill, daring, and charm made him a hero among the British. It was no different in Mexico; and in Argentina, with its millions of citizens of Italian origin, his popularity was second only to Fangio's. In Italy he was the pride and joy of a country which at that time had no shortage of racing heroes to idolize. His name had a magic quality throughout the world.

Like many, if not most, racing drivers, Ascari was intensely superstitious, and he had some sound encouragement for being so. On one occasion, when he and Villoresi were embarking for the South American season, Ascari stopped on the gangplank of the ship. "I have a bad feeling about this voyage," he said, "and I'm not going." Villoresi laughed at his comrade's hunch but it was only a near miracle that saved Villoresi's life when the ship sank.

It is strange that Ascari seemed to read no warning into his accident at Monaco on May 22, 1955. He was married, had two children, and had been set up in business by Lancia, whose new GP car he was driving. Through a sheer error in judgment he lost control during the GP and plunged into the harbor. By the grace of God a couple of skin divers were at just that spot and saved him.

Four days later he went to Monza, "just to watch the practice that's going on," he told his wife, Miretta. Of course he wouldn't drive. He was so superstitious about his old blue crash helmet that he treated it like a holy relic and, after Monaco, it was in a shop for repair.

Ascari was still suffering from contusions acquired in the accident. He went to the pit of his friend and pupil, Eugenio Castellotti, where he ate lunch. He never would eat before driving. Then Castellotti took a few laps in a new, 3-liter Ferrari and came in with a new record of 2M 4s. Ascari was still smarting from the *brutta figura* (the bad public impression) that he had made at Monaco. Perhaps he felt that a fine new lap record would show the world that Monaco had just been an off day, and what Castellotti could do Ascari could improve upon with ease. He borrowed his friend's helmet and the car went out of control on entering the Lesmo Curve. He was thirty-seven.

The first person to reach the wreckage was Villoresi. He gave up driving. Ascari's son, Tonino, has begun to race.

In the days when drivers were meant to be seen, Alberto Ascari was one of the most spectacular. Here he drives a 1951 Ferrari on the Modena Circuit in Italy.

Mike Hawthorn

1958

John Michael Hawthorn was Britain's first winner of the World Championship of Drivers. He promptly retired, "glad still to be alive," and within six weeks he was dead. His career was one of great heights and depths.

Mike was born in Mexborough, Yorkshire, on April 10, 1929. His father, Leslie, was a super-tuner of motorcycle engines and when Mike was two the family moved to Farnham to be handy to the Brooklands Track near London. Hawthorn was attracted to the sports cars and racing cars that came to his father's garage, and not to the bikes. His father shared and encouraged Mike's enthusiasm and in 1950 bought a pair of prewar sports Rileys — an 1100 and a 1500 — for them to go racing with together. The following year Mike was doing most of the driving of both cars and did so well that he was offered a new Formula Two Cooper-Bristol to handle. He drove it in the opening event of the British 1951 season, the annual Easter Meeting at Goodwood. He won the Open Formula race outright and won wide and immediate recognition as a driver of Grand Prix caliber.

This early success was further enhanced wherever Mike and the Cooper-Bristol raced. In England and on the Continent, this was the fantastic combination that harassed the big Ferraris, occasionally beat them, and usually beat everything else. It was so simple and so sudden. At the end of the 1951 season Enzo Ferrari invited Mike to drive for him. Not since Mercedes-Benz had sought out Richard Seaman in the 1930's had such an honor come from across the Channel. Mike, of course, was in heaven.

His first race for Ferrari was the GP of Argentina in January of 1953.

177

Mike Hawthorn achieved racing immortality as the first British Grand Prix champion.

He finished fourth, behind Ascari, Villoresi, and Gonzales. A week later, in the GP of Buenos Aires, he was third, behind Farina and Villoresi. Back in Europe after that, in France's Pau GP, he was second behind Ascari. At Silverstone he won the sports car race in a 4.1 Ferrari *and* the Formula Two *Daily Express* Trophy Race in a 2-liter Ferrari. No driver ever rose more meteorically.

Up to this time it had been accepted almost universally that it took many years of experience and real maturity to make a front-rank GP driver. Mike had just turned twenty-four and, not even halfway into his first season in the real "big time," had taken his place among the masters.

The French GP at Reims that year was one of the greatest races of all time. Heading the twenty-four-car field were the Maseratis of Fangio, Gonzales, Bonetto, and Marimon, and the Ferraris of Ascari, Villoresi, Farina, and Hawthorn. For almost the final half of the 312-mile race it was Fangio and Hawthorn battling wheel-to-wheel and hammering down the lap record again and again. Rarely has such a duel been seen in racing history, and the emotion-wracked crowd went mad when Hawthorn took Fangio on the final turn and flashed across the line as the victor.

178

"He will be world champion in two years," said Enzo Ferrari, assuming that Mike would be driving his cars. But for the rest of the season Mike's best placings were thirds at the Nürburgring and at Berne.

The next year, 1954, was bitter. First, Britain's yellow press found that Mike had never done military service and sold millions of newspapers by smearing the new hero. This went on for months until all charges were retired in the light of official revelation of the grave state of his kidneys.

Then, in the Syracuse GP, he crashed, was badly burned, and was hospitalized for many weeks. Just as he was prepared to start in the 24 Hours of Le Mans, his father was killed in a road accident. Mike seriously considered retreating to a more calm way of life but finished off the season with second places in the British, German, and Italian GP's and won the Spanish GP, which closed the season.

In 1955 he joined the British Vanwall team for Formula One and the Jaguar team for sports car racing. The Vanwalls still needed much development, and it was an empty year for Mike in the Grands Prix. In sports cars it was something else. It was his Jaguar that was in front of Lance Macklin's Austin-Healey that was struck by Pierre Levegh's Mercedes-Benz before the Mercedes careened, flaming, into the crowd. Much of the Continental press blamed Hawthorn (who, with co-driver Ivor Bueb, went on to win the race) for having caused the accident that led to the disaster. Eventually a French tribunal cleared all involved parties of any direct guilt.

In 1956 Mike signed to drive Formula One for BRM. It was another unripe cause, as the Vanwall had been. In 1957 he rejoined Ferrari but took only a second in the German GP and a third in the British. Then came *the* year.

Mike continued with Ferrari. With one championship race left to go he had won only the French GP but had scored seconds in the Belgian,

British, Portuguese, and Italian Grandes Epreuves. Stirling Moss had three firsts and a second to his credit. As the points stood, if he were to win the GP of Morocco in October *and* turn the fastest lap *and* if Hawthorn should not finish second, Moss would win the championship. Moss did his part magnificently but Phil Hill, running interference for his Ferrari teammate, let Mike into second place at the finish. Thus he became champion by the margin of a single point. He announced his retirement in December, and on January 22, 1959, his road car slammed into a tree and he was instantly killed.

For several years Mike was the most colorful member of what used to be a highly colorful crew. He smoked, drank, reveled, was the life of a million parties and the instigator of a million riotous pranks, from dismantling hotels to conducting garbage-can races through the streets of sleeping towns at midnight. When he won the championship, however, he carried the honor with decorum.

He was no serene stylist in a racing car. His six-foot frame towered in the cockpit, in spite of his manner of hunching over the wheel. He drove with teeth clenched and bared or with his lips set in a grim line, thrashing at the wheel and drifting his turns superbly. He was always meticulously fair.

Mike never showed any but the most casual interest in the money side of racing. He drove and he lived for fun, for the sheer joy of it all, and long before his retirement he became embittered with the commercialism that invaded the sport. He wanted to get out of it because the old, carefree group he had known was being replaced by business executives in bucket seats.

After it was over Stirling Moss said, "Mike said that in his opinion Ascari was the fastest driver, Fangio the most intelligent, and Nuvolari the greatest; I would like to add one more name to this short list: Hawthorn, the greatest fighter of them all."

Jack Brabham, O.B.E.

1959, 1960, 1966

Among his many distinctions, Jack Brabham has driven more Formula One Grands Prix than any other man. The 1966 GP of Mexico was his eighty-third, finally putting him beyond French veteran Maurice Trintignant. This statistic is interesting in itself, but its real meaning, of course, is that Brabham has a store of this type of racing experience and a knowledge of the world's Grand Prix circuits that are almost without equal. These blend well with some of Jack's other assets.

He is an expert mechanic and machinist. He is one of the best test drivers and development engineers of racing vehicles in the world in addition to being one of the best drivers, period. He is endowed with appalling physical and mental energy, *all* of which is devoted to the single purpose of racing. His judgment, whether in planning his driving strategy for a single race or his design strategy for a year or more, is direct, lucid and penetratingly simple. "That wonderful Australian craftiness," John Cooper calls it, with frank and cheerful admiration.

That it's a very smart way of thinking is reflected in Jack's three championships, his attainment of the Order of the British Empire, and the fact that, while winning the 1966 Formula One championship magnificently, he also found time to absolutely steamroller Formula Two, winning the British and French championships in that category. To make all this more marvelous and unprecedented, he scored these victories not only as a driver but also as the constructor of the cars that bore his name. Fabulous is the word.

Along with all this the quiet Aussie also finds time and energy to direct several important businesses, one of which is called Motor Racing

In addition to being one of the truly great drivers, Jack Brabham, of Australia, is also a highly talented designer and builder of racing cars.

Developments Limited. Jack's MRD is history's largest constructor of open-wheel racing cars (Formulas One, Two, Three, and Junior). By the end of 1966 it had produced and sold over 250 such machines in far-flung parts of the world. For a living, dynamic monument to energy, enterprise, determination, dedication, and achievement one doesn't have to look beyond Brabham.

He is tall, black haired and solidly built but far too serious to contribute any flashy showmanship to the racing scene. He is shy, modest, and reserved, neither smokes nor drinks, and likes very simple food. Instead of being brilliant he is steady, the sort of man who seems to be dormant for years, while he is always working toward his goal. Brabham's type is that of the consistent champion. Inevitably, then, he is compared with Fangio.

Jack was born in Sydney on October 2, 1926. He began working as an auto mechanic at sixteen and had his own garage at twenty. Then, immediately after World War II, he became interested in what Americans call Midget racing and what Australians call Speedway racing. Jack built a Midget for a visiting American driver. The Yank moved on, and Jack,

182

left with the machine, took to campaigning it himself. He hacked away as a Midget driver and mechanic for six years, during which he won the championships of New South Wales and of Australia on two occasions.

In 1951 Jack responded to the lure of road racing and invested in a 500 cc Cooper and then in a 2-liter Cooper-Bristol. Again his class showed in long strings of victories and in more regional championships. Then European competitors began arriving in Australia. One look at their sophistication of design and the quality of their equipment convinced Brabham that if he wanted to advance he would have to go to Europe.

He arrived in England in 1955, made his way through an assortment of privately owned machinery, and then, in 1957, joined the Cooper factory team. During 1958 he made a cautious start in Formula One, winning second places in a pair of non-championship events behind Moss and Hawthorn and ahead of many excellent drivers. Then in 1959 he began to emerge as a driver of the first international rank. His first place in the Monaco and British GP's, plus a second in the Dutch, and thirds in the French and Italian gave him the championship by a four-point margin. At that time he was not impressed by the championship and said, "I suppose it's a good idea, but it's a bit of a worry. From the driver's point of view it takes a lot of enjoyment out of racing. But it does create a lot of public interest."

In 1960 Jack racked up a spectacular five first places in a row — in the Dutch, Belgian, French, British, and Portuguese Grands Prix — which gave him his second championship by a very convincing nine points.

That October he and John Cooper did violence to the course of racing history by appearing at Indianapolis with a 2.5-liter rear-engined Cooper-Climax. Although the little car's power plant had only about 60 percent of the displacement of the big Offies and although Jack never had seen the track before, he lapped the oval at 144.834 MPH. This was within five MPH of the "fantastic" lap record which Jim Hurtubise had set the previous May. The racing world was shaken to its roots, and the death knell of the traditional Indianapolis roadster was sounded.

In 1961, with no proper British engines for the new 1.5-liter formula, Jack's thoughts turned to building his own cars. At the end of a dull season he severed professional relations with his old friend, John Cooper, and established Brabham Racing Developments (which became MRD in 1965). He began building Formula Three cars and in 1962 introduced his first car for Formula One, powered by a Coventry Climax V8. By the end of the season it was sufficiently developed to be able to finish fourth in the last two big events of the year. Thus Jack was the first man in history to win championship points in a car of his own construction.

From 1961 through 1965 Jack lay low in Formula One, winning not a single championship point. But he was magnificently prepared for 1966 and was far ahead of everyone but Ferrari. His Brabham-Repco cars consisted of the previous year's light, simple, *and* fully developed chassis, plus an engine based on the Buick V8 aluminum block and using Repco single overhead camshaft cylinder heads. Here was a GP car that cost perhaps as little as $7000 to build, in contrast to several times that for all the others. During practice at Monaco at the start of the season, I pointed out to Jack that his stock-block approach might start another revolution.

"I'm afraid not," he said. "We have an advantage in being ready *now*, but as the others become developed we will hurt for power. I see this engine as being good for just this season . . . with luck. Repco is building us an entirely new one for next year."

At this moment Fangio strolled over and greeted us. "Say," laughed Jack, "ask him if he thinks I'm too old for this nonsense."

184

I did and Fangio laughed back, "All I can say is that I was thirty-nine when I *started out* in this nonsense."

At forty Jack hardly showed signs of senility. In his charging, slightly erratic style, rarely taking the same line through a turn, he won the 1966 championship by a margin of 17 points. And what did he think of it? "Well, I'd like to win it three more times, just to be one-up on Juan Manuel." Jack came within a scant five points of winning the championship again in 1967. He was beaten only by a driver whom he had trained, in a car which he had designed and built.

Phil Hill

1961

Phil Hill won his first Grand Prix race at Monza in 1960. A year later he won the Italian GP again and, with it, the championship. He is, of course, the first American driver to achieve the world title.

Phillip T. Hill, Jr., was born in Santa Monica, California, in 1928. Perhaps one of the difficulties of his life, in view of the career he chose, was that he was born into an old, aristocratic family — one of refinement, respectability, social position, and decorum. His mother was an accomplished musician and composer, and his father was a distinguished civic leader in the well-to-do seaside community. Their son was born with serious responsibilities.

When Phil became a "fanatic" about cars almost in his infancy there was no alarm. When, at age twelve, he turned up with his very own battered, ten-dollar Model-T Ford, he was just ahead of his years. He was too young to drive on the streets, but there was a small dirt track nearby where he was allowed to trundle around to his heart's content. When he began driving street roadsters that, after all, was normal for the younger set. When he began going off to speedfests on the Southern California dry lakes it was felt that this adolescent interest also would pass.

None of this is prying into Phil's private life. He is about as self-analytical as a person can be and speaks of his background with detachment and insight.

He had no conscious inkling of what he wanted to do in life when he entered the University of Southern California. For lack of anything better to do he majored in business administration and found it to be a total bore. Then in his Junior year he became involved in Midget racing circles. To his parents' horror Phil chucked his formal education to be-

Phil Hill is the first and, so far, the only American to win the world championship.

come a mechanic on an Offenhauser Midget crew. For two years he often worked seven nights a week at this job, learning a lot that they don't teach at USC.

In 1948 Phil saw one of the first MC TC's to reach Southern California. He loved the car on sight, bought one, and began racing it on dirt tracks in a hell-bent, blindly aggressive, win-or-bust way. When road racing began on the West Coast he was one of the pioneer contestants. He used up one TC, then another, and then stepped up to a modified Jaguar XK-120. In this car he scored his first important road-racing victory at Pebble Beach, California, in 1950. Then came an old but superb 2.9-liter Alfa and then the first of a series of Ferraris.

His whole life had come to center around racing. But racing was thoroughly alien to the self-image to which he had been taught to aspire.

187

He developed a nice catalog of symptoms, including an ulcer, and, at the beginning of 1954, gave up racing on doctor's orders.

This self-denial lasted for ten months. Then he was offered his third ride in the 1900-mile Mexican Road Race in a Ferrari. With his good friend Richie Ginther as co-pilot Phil drove fabulously and finished second over-all. It was one of the finest races of his career. He recognized it as such and it was *the* turning point in his life. If he could acquit himself well among the finest drivers in the world, then there was a career for him in racing after all. With this decision made his old inner conflicts began to vanish.

Phil went to work on polishing his style in races all over the Western Hemisphere. He got steadily better, and at the start of the 1956 season he was invited to join the Ferrari factory's sports-car racing team. He jumped at this, of course, and, in racing under European conditions, he began to find such sweet rewards as public honor and inner fulfillment. Then in 1958 Ferrari started him out in Formula One at Buenos Aires. He was third at Monza that year and also at Casablanca. Mike Hawthorn singled him out as a coming champion.

Driving in Formula One in 1959 Phil was second at Reims and Monza and third at the Avus; in 1960 he won at Monza and was third at Monaco. Then in 1961 he was first at Spa, second at Zandvoort and Aintree, and third at Monaco and the Nürburgring. At the start of the Italian Grand Prix Phil's Ferrari teammate, Wolfgang von Trips, had 30 championship points. Phil was next with 24, but with this race and the United States GP yet to go a great deal could still happen.

On the second lap at Monza, in the Parabolic Curve, von Trips was crowded against Jim Clark's Lotus. The Ferrari flew out of control and into the crowd; von Trips and fifteen spectators were killed. The tragedy was not announced and the race went on, with Phil the winner and therefore irrevocably the new champion. The title was precious to him, but

188

the lives of others were infinitely more so. There was no joy in the victory for anyone.

Phil considered giving up racing then and there, but finally decided to continue as before. Then, in 1963, his contract with Ferrari was not renewed.

Therefore he followed the former Ferrari group which had founded the new ATS firm. There were florid hopes for the ATS Grand Prix car and when it ran properly the Number One driver left no doubt that his ability had lost none of its edge. He remained loyal to the terms of his contract until the whole effort was dropped.

Phil Hill stands five feet ten, has brown eyes and hair, and the body of an athlete, which he is careful to keep in top condition. He is extremely alive intellectually and is devoted to fine music and to fine vintage cars, of which he had seven at the last count. He is intense by nature but much of his nervousness of past years has been replaced by deeply felt self-assurance. Since the disappointing ATS experience he has concentrated upon sports-car racing, his old love. He is frequently called upon as a consultant and much of the quality of the racing photography in the MGM film *Grand Prix* exists as a result of his influence and guidance.

Graham Hill

1962

YOU TOO CAN BE A RACING DRIVER was the gist of a small ad in a small automotive magazine that someone had tossed in a corner of the shop. Graham Hill, twenty-four-year-old technician at Smith's, the big British automotive accessory firm, did not know how to drive and never had shown any interest in cars. Some uncanny instinct caused him to focus on this ad and ask himself, "Why not?" Then he trundled out to Brands Hatch and paid a hard-earned $2.80 for the privilege of taking four laps in a tired 500-cc Cooper. Nine years later he was the Champion Driver of the World.

Graham was born into a modest London family on February 15, 1929. He left school at sixteen to serve a long apprenticeship at Smith's. He bought a motorcycle and engaged in field trials until he fell off and broke a thigh. He served two years in the Royal Navy and became a boiler-room specialist, then returned to Smith's as a paid employe, working on the development of such products as magnetic clutches and car heaters. He recently wrote, "By training I am, I suppose, an engineer."

The one ride in the little Cooper fired Graham with the determination to become a racing driver. His only connection with the sport was the ride-vendor at Brands, to whom Graham attached himself by working for the man a half day per week, without pay. This entrepreneur passed from the scene very quickly but the void was filled by another, who had two such cars and a plan to establish a proper "racing drivers' school." This time Graham offered his services as a full-time mechanic without pay, and landed the job. He quit his position at Smith's, filed for unemployment insurance ($4.50 per week), and threw himself into his new

190

Graham Hill, second British champion of the world. The marks on his helmet are the insignia of his old rowing club.

career. The dole payments barely kept him in carfare but he lived with his parents; his mother went along with his plan, and domestic harmony was preserved by sparing his father from the facts.

Graham wanted to drive, not just to straighten bent machinery. He seized his chance one day when his employer gave him the additional unpaid duty of "telling the chaps how to drive." Graham pleaded that he would be a much more effective instructor if *he* knew what it was like to drive the cars. He was given a few rides, but disappointingly few, and so he drifted on. He didn't have much to lose.

By this time, late 1954, Graham had gained considerable self-confidence. One day he engaged Colin Chapman in conversation at the track. The chat was cordial and ended with an invitation for Graham to visit the Lotus "works" — a lean-to then — when he had a free moment. This resulted in Graham picking up an occasional stint of wrench-twisting for $2.80 per day.

He also worked as a mechanic for a couple of private owners of racing cars and in 1955 drove a few races in one of them, a Type C Jaguar. Then Chapman took him on as a full-time mechanic, with the promise

Even world champions sometimes drive badly, as Hill demonstrated repeatedly in Mexico in 1964, when trying to stay ahead of Lorenzo Bandini.

of an occasional ride. The first of these materialized early in the 1956 season in the boss's personal 1100-cc sports Lotus. Once more the action took place at Brands Hatch and to everyone's amazement Graham won the 1100-cc event. Then he drove the same car in the 1500-cc race, finished second, and broke the 1500-cc lap record, which had been set by Chapman. For some reason his boss grounded him and, early in 1957, Graham went back to free lancing.

It was toward the end of this Chapman phase that Hill bought his second car for personal transport. The first had been a small used Morris, which Graham acquired in 1953, while he was still innocent of any driving experience. The car was wrecked two months later. The second machine was a well-used 1929 Austin Seven, which he bought from Mrs. Chapman for a song. During the two years he drove it he spent practically nothing on its upkeep. When its brakes gave out he commonly stopped the car by grinding its tires against curbs. To quote author Dennis May, "The main requirements for racing success, in Graham's opinion, are anticipation, concentration, and determination, and he's found nothing develops these attributes faster than driving a practically brakeless 1929 Austin Seven."

After some very modest racing successes Graham was pleasantly

192

startled toward the end of 1957 by an out-of-the-blue invitation from Chapman to return to Lotus as a team driver. Even with allowances made for the inferiority of the Lotus GP cars of that vintage, Graham did nothing memorable in the 1958 and 1959 seasons. There was one possible exception: in the 1958 GP of Monaco he started in the last row and, due to the systematic failure of the cars in front of him, found himself in fourth position before his engine also expired.

In 1960, however, Raymond Mays invited Graham to join the BRM team. Mays's praise for his choice was rather faint: "I felt he was a driver to be reckoned with and to be encouraged. . . . I should also regard him as a good team man."

During that year and the next Graham did not add to the single championship point he had picked up by finishing sixth and next-to-last at Monza in 1958. But he was quietly acquiring experience and in 1962 he blossomed spectacularly, placing second in the Belgian and United States Grands Prix, and winning outright in the Dutch, German, Italian, and South African. It was in this last race, when Clark seemed certain to win the championship, that Graham won it by "default," to use his own word. But his over-all performance that season was undeniably of real championship quality.

Ever since that convincing coming-of-age, Graham has been consistently in the vanguard of competition. He was second in points in 1963; and in 1964 he was leading in points when, during the final race of the season, he got sideways one time too many, drifted into Bandini and lost his chance once more. When he referred to his "just plain bad driving" the British press turned this into criticism of the Italian driver who had done his best to get around the bizarre obstacles Hill had put in his way. In 1965 he was second in points once more. His 1966 GP season was not good due mainly, no doubt, to teething troubles with the new BRM H-16 engine. But it did give him a fine and very lucrative victory at

Indianapolis. At the end of the 1966 season he left BRM to return to Team Lotus.

Graham has mastered a machine-like smoothness of style, which is in keeping with his physical appearance. The handsome six-footer has the frozen countenance of one of the Queen's own guard. Dennis May speaks of his "curious impassivity of expression, like well-set blanc-mange [gelatin] . . . he says it [his face] becomes so rigid during races that it takes a conscious effort to limber it into mobility afterwards." Hill reminds Henry Manny of "a stuffed racing driver."

He also tends to be very calm and sometimes reveals a sly wit in his speech. For example: "Funnily enough, this business of travelling along the edge of disaster is probably the key to why drivers want to go racing in the first place, and I suppose there's some psychological reason for that."

Possibly there is, but there is no questioning the fact that Graham Hill is one of the fastest, smoothest, slickest, and steadiest of his breed today. His story proves that you don't have to be born a car nut to become a racing driver . . . even one of the best.

Jim Clark, O.B.E.

1963, 1965

Jim Clark was one of the phenomenal driving talents of all time. There was nothing spectacular about his style. He drove in a very efficient, standard manner, but the lines he followed seemed to be tighter, shorter, and therefore quicker than those of all the others. When he had anything like a competitive car he was *the* pace-setter, the man whose lap times all other contestants would have liked to have been able to equal or, at least, to approach. Even with cars that were running badly due to engine or running-gear defects he was repeatedly a top finisher. He had a gift for nursing sick machinery and in spite of his consistently outstanding speeds he was notoriously easy on tires. He was at the peak of his skill and a millionaire in his profession at age 32 when his career was ended in a crash.

Jim had no engineering background but was gifted with a rare ability to sense what goes on inside a machine. As Number One driver for Team Lotus he had his choice of cars for each race. He usually practiced in each of the available machines. The one he chose may have been the slowest of the lot but it was frequently the most reliable and the eventual winner.

In addition to this sort of sixth sense for machinery Jim had consistently good judgment. In other words, he was an intelligent driver.

He also was a born fighter with, obviously, a will to win. The same can be said of Lotus cultivator Colin Chapman, and the two men — super driver and super car-builder — made a unique and powerful team. Jim's judgment was nicely illustrated by the fact that he resisted some very enticing offers in order to preserve this remarkable working relationship. Chapman is not the world's easiest man with whom to get along, but Jim,

195

Normally shy and silent, Scotsman Jim Clark was one of the most consistent great driving talents of all time.

because he had no need to drive for money and because of his stupendous talent, could and did treat Chapman as an equal.

Jim was born in Scotland in 1937. His father is a wealthy sheep farmer, and Jim was raised to follow in the paternal footsteps. He had his own large farm near Duns, Berwickshire, in the southeast Scottish Lowlands, loved that serene life, and spent much of his free time on the farm. At home the brown-haired, brown-eyed, 5-foot 6-inch, two-time champion tramped his meadows in work boots and blue overalls, carrying a shepherd's hooked staff. He was an authentic, practicing, Scottish sheep farmer.

During his school years Jim was fond of and very good at track sports and hockey. At fifteen his interest in automobile racing began to grow. Rustic Berwickshire happened to have its own very dynamic racing team, called the Border Reivers. It was, and is, composed of a group of local farmers and garage owners, headed by farmer Ian Scott-Watson. Jim, of course, gravitated to this group and was given the greatest encouragement and guidance by Scott-Watson. He was nineteen when this influential person gave him his first racing ride in a DKW sedan.

Jim's first personal car was a Sunbeam sedan, which he raced and soon replaced with a Triumph TR-3 and then with a Porsche coupé. In 1957 he won his first reasonably important race at Charterhall in the Porsche and was given Scott-Watson's Lotus Elite to drive. The following year he continued racing the Elite and was able to enrich his education at the wheel of a Lister-Jaguar that the Border Reivers had acquired. In 1959 he realized that he was capable of driving really fast, and he began giving serious thought to a future in Formula One.

He contacted Chapman, who signed him for the 1960 season to drive in Formula Two and Formula Junior. He was so good that Chapman gave him his first Formula One ride in the Dutch GP. He finished fifth in the Belgian and the French, and third in the Portuguese. Driving only a partial season, the rookie nevertheless finished it with 8 championship points. He co-drove an Aston-Martin with Roy Salvadori at Le Mans and finished third; and he shared the 1960 Formula Junior championship with Trevor Taylor.

For 1961 Jim was elevated to Number Two rank on Team Lotus. Chapman was still in search of a really competitive design combination. The cars were not performing very well but Jim finished third in the Dutch and French GP's and fourth in the German, which gave him 11 championship points for that season. He had offers from other *équipes* but chose to stick with Lotus.

In 1962 he replaced Innes Ireland as Number One on the team. At Spa he achieved his first GP victory, to which he added wins in the British and American GP's. The championship would be decided by the last race of the season, the South African. Jim had it all-but-won when the famous oil plug fell out of his engine and the title passed to Graham Hill.

In 1963 the combination was perfect. The semi-monocoque Lotus and the Coventry-Climax V8 were working exceedingly well and enabled Jim to reveal his full powers. He won the Belgian, Dutch, French, and British GP's in succession, was second in the German, first again in the Italian, third at Watkins Glen, then finished the season with firsts in Mexico and South Africa. He had amassed 54 championship points, while second-place Graham Hill had 29. In many of these races Clark was untouchable, leading from start to finish. He might well have had even more points had he not missed the Monaco GP in order to drive at Indianapolis. There, because he observed the yellow "hold-positions" flag when others did not, he finished only second. He went on to Milwaukee where, driving against the same basic field, he won. This put him fourth in USAC championship points. At Indianapolis the man who was about to become champion of the world was voted Rookie of the Year.

In 1964 Jim was only third in championship points standing. Then in 1965 it was the old story again, only more so. He was the outright winner of six of the ten Grands Prix. And this time he *won* at Indianapolis.

Except for his win at Watkins Glen, 1966 was a year of almost no achievements for Clark and Lotus, mainly due to the lack of preparation of the H-16 BRM engine, which Lotus then used.

When he won the championship in 1963 Jim was entirely indifferent

Clark, Lotus-mounted, demonstrated his flawless style on the Nürburgring in 1965.

to it, stating that he drove for enjoyment and not for glory. In 1965 it was otherwise. British critics sniped at him for abandoning Monaco "in favor of Indianapolis gold." This time his fighting spirit and Scottish pride were outraged and he craved the championship, just to show that he could win it in spite of missing one of the classic events.

Jim Clark was a quiet, retiring introvert, as many good racing drivers and farmers are. He was modest and reserved, was no mixer at all, but was almost harshly frank, candid, and honest. That he was a very nervous person was indicated by his gnawed-to-the-quick fingernails. He didn't smoke, drank moderately, avoided strangers and crowds, but was thoroughly, boyishly sociable in company that he had learned to accept.

Clark began the 1967 season late in a car that was as untried as it was brilliant: the Lotus-Ford. With it he won four races, double the number which were won by champion Denis Hulme and runner-up Jack Brabham. The 1968 season was off to a promising start both for Lotus and its Number One driver as Clark won the first GP of the year at Kyalami, South Africa, raising his total victories to twenty-five, one more than even the legendary Fangio had achieved.

On April 7, 1968, Clark drove a Formula Two Lotus in the German trophy race counting toward the European Formula Two championship at Hockenheim Motordrom near Heidelberg. His car was in seventh place in the first of two scheduled heats of the contest. The track was wet. As it roared down the straight at a speed some observers estimated at 175 MPH, Clark's Lotus veered suddenly, somersaulted into the woods alongside the track, and smashed to pieces against a tree. Clark died instantly in the crash. Fellow drivers who observed the crash felt that mechanical failure must have been to blame for the accident, for they could not believe a driver of Clark's skill could have made a mistake under the circumstances, despite the wet track. Track officials said the car was so badly damaged that the chances of determining the cause of the accident were remote.

John Surtees

1964

In John Surtees' story we have, among other things, an ideal example of the extremes of justice that are inherent in the championship-points system as it has existed to date. Under it, as in boxing, the world title can be won by a decisive display of overwhelming superiority or it can be won by a TKO that satisfies and convinces hardly anyone. Surtees has won world titles both ways.

Next to being an astronaut I find it hard to imagine any other pursuit that requires as much sheer bravery as racing big Grand Prix motorcycles. Cornering at 140 MPH and more with just two tiny patches of rubber between yourself and almost certain oblivion calls for extraordinary courage. A bit of dirt or a few drops of oil or any interruption of power transmission to the driving wheel can be fatal. Cornering all the way over on the foot-pegs is only part of it. There is no structure whatsoever to protect you; on the contrary, the machine bristles with projections that can impale you.

Many fine and some master drivers have come up through the motorcycle racing ranks, partly because the margin for error in this kind of racing is almost nonexistant. It is a matchless school for the development of the whole gamut of physical and mental skills, including the ability to make faultless judgments instantaneously, continuously, and without exception.

Surtees is so superb in this awesome form of competition that he won the absolute — 500 cc — world motorcycle title not once, but for three years in succession. He also won four world titles in the 350 cc class, the two-wheel equivalent of Formula Two. For an incredible two and

John Surtees of England was world champion on motorcycles before he won the Grand Prix championship for Ferrari in 1964.

one-half years he was never beaten in a championship event. This is evidence of almost unbelievable skill.

John was born in London in 1934. His father, Jack, had been a famous motorcycle racer in his youth and operated a large dealership for bikes. John naturally grew up on them. His father taught him the techniques of racing in his very early teens, including caution, conservatism, and a healthy appreciation for the God-given instinct of fear.

John's formal racing career began when he was fifteen. He rode from success to success until he joined the Italian MV Agusta factory team in 1956. With these four-cylinder, dual-overhead-camshaft thoroughbreds, he found the combination that made him unbeatable, the Fangio of the motorcycle world. At home he was a national hero and a legend.

In 1960 he decided to give automobile racing a try. In his first practice runs at Silverstone in May he was pronounced "fantastic" — as he indeed was — and the home press immediately announced the discovery of tomorrow's Grand Prix champion. Everyone rushed him and expected the ultimate from him overnight.

Surtees, the consummate professional, hated this. All he wanted was to be left alone to gather experience in his methodical and cautious way and to start driving really fast only when he felt himself to be fully in command of this new art. He had time to drive only a few races in 1960 because he was involved primarily with wrapping up the world motorcycle championship one more, final time. But in the British GP this rank newcomer could not avoid finishing second to Brabham and in the Portuguese GP, as we have seen, the experts judged and announced that he had arrived.

John did not agree and he announced that his sole aim for the 1961 season was to get experience on four wheels. He gave up bike racing and drove Coopers for Reg Parnell. He deliberately took it easy, learning about the behavior of Formula One cars and studying the methods of those whom he acknowledged as his superiors.

He was not happy with the Coopers, had his own ideas for an improved suspension layout, and contributed them to the design of a Formula One Lola which he drove in 1962. There was plenty of sorting out to be done with the new car, but he did finish second in the British and German GP's and fourth in championship points for the season.

That season had been a rout for Ferrari. Surtees accepted Ferrari's invitation to join the factory team and got off to a brilliant start with sports car victories in the Sebring 12 Hours and the Nürburgring 1000 kilometers, co-driving with Scarfiotti and Mairesse. The Formula One cars seldom ran well, however, and his only good position in a championship race was his first at the Nürburgring.

In 1964 the transmission of John's Ferrari failed at Monaco. He was second in the Dutch GP, his engine gave up in the Belgian GP, an oil line broke in the French GP, and he took third in the British GP. Then his luck improved. He won the German, went out with broken suspension at Zeltweg, won at Monza, and was second at Watkins Glen. This motley assortment gave him 35 championship points when he came to the last starting grid of the season, Mexico City. Graham Hill led with 39 points and Clark had 32. But this was Clark's own race; he had won it twice before and he, Chapman, and most others expected him to win it again.

As it worked out Graham Hill, driving maniacally, made light contact with Bandini's Ferrari. This caused Hill to bump the guard rail and bend his BRM's exhaust pipes. The resulting loss of time wiped out his hopes for the race and for the championship. Meanwhile, Clark was lapping practically everybody and by Lap 56 was more than a minute ahead of Surtees. But on the 63rd of the 65 laps he rolled into his pit with an engine that had lost its last drop of oil. Gurney found himself in the lead and on the final lap Bandini, in the much faster 12-cylinder Ferrari, slowed and let Surtees' V8 into second place and the world title.

John did not win another Formula One championship event until the Belgian GP in 1966. He did slightly better in sports car racing but Enzo Ferrari's esteem for his Number One driver began to decay no later than early 1965. The disenchantment was at least mutual, and John and Enzo agreed to tear up their contract in May, 1966.

John made a fairly quick realignment with John Cooper and, driving Cooper-Maseratis, was second in the German, third in the United States, and first in the Mexican GP's. With a car that was new to him he had hit a new stride.

The Ferrari environment, not known for its internal harmony, certainly did not provide calm, calculating Surtees with a good working combination. With Honda of Japan he has been invaluable as development engineer, test driver, and driver. The combination began to click in September of 1967 when, in a new and untried Honda, he won the Grand Prix of Italy at Monza.

Stirling Moss, O.B.E.

Uncrowned Champion

The man is much more than just one of the two or three finest racing drivers of all time; he is a towering figure in racing history. This is because the brilliance of his achievements and the example he set shook the racing world to its core. He demonstrated what *could* be done. The whole United Kingdom — and an amazed world — watched in awe, then followed his lead. He contributed strongly to Britain's golden age in Grand Prix racing.

It is hard to remember today that when Moss began his solitary crusade to bring new excellence to racing there were no British drivers of the first rank. Now they dominate the sport. It is hard to remember the countless breakthroughs he made; for example, his victory for Vanwall at Pescara in 1957 was the first win by a British car on foreign soil in thirty-four years. He always led, always pointed the way.

It is one of Fate's great ironies that, in spite of Moss's utterly staggering achievements, he and the championship always managed to elude each other. As an anonymous writer has said, "The world championship is diminished by Moss not having won it, rather than the other way around."

As a matter of fact, the existing points system was recognized as being defective and was changed. Under the present system Moss would have been champion in 1956 and 1958. But if he did not win the title he hacked out a legacy for the world and, above all, for his countrymen. For a man who is passionately patriotic this is no mean reward.

Moss was born in London on September 17, 1929. His father, Alfred Moss, studied at Indiana Dental College and drove Frontenac-Ford race cars in the Indianapolis "500" on two occasions; until recently the elder

It is generally agreed that only two other drivers in racing history — Tazio Nuvolari and Juan Fangio — have surpassed the performance record of Stirling Moss.

Moss was the only Englishman to have made two starts at Indy. On returning to England Alfred Moss, dentist, continued to take part in races, rallies, and trials, and he married a girl who was good at the same sports. Thus Stirling grew up in a racing-oriented environment.

His parents let him have his first car — a stripped-down Austin Seven — when he was eleven. He learned to drive it on a rugged course over the fields around their farm. At fifteen he had a Morgan 3-wheeler, at seventeen an MG and then a BMW 328, and at eighteen a 500 cc Cooper. Until early 1954 he drove 500 cc and 1000 cc one-man cars and a disappointing collection of HWM's, and a Cooper-Alta. Then, at the start of the season, his father presented him with a very nice gift — a 2.5-liter Formula One Maserati. This was his first Grand Prix car and also the first potential winner that he had yet had.

From this moment his rise was meteoric. He outperformed the factory Maserati drivers with the result that the factory took him on as Number One driver. In 1955 he joined the Mercedes-Benz team as second to Fangio, the crowned champion. In 1956 he returned to Maserati as Number One, and in 1957 joined Vanwall in the same capacity. In the 1959 season he began his policy of driving non-factory cars, and his driving career ended with the terrible accident at Goodwood early in 1962. That he survived it was remarkable.

205

Moss's best years in terms of championship point standings were, rather predictably, those he spent driving on factory teams, where the latest refinements are always to be found. In 1955, 1956, and 1957 he was second in points to Fangio's first. In 1958 he was second again, trailing Hawthorn by a single point. He finished third in points for each of the next three years, which had to have something to do with the competitiveness of the machines he had to drive. This was no one's fault but his own. He is not the sort of man not to have had his own excellent reasons for choosing independently owned cars.

There never was a man like Moss and there never will be another. As a human being, as an athlete, and as a very special type of intellect he stands by himself.

Once, during a week that we spent together, I asked him why he or any other driver in the ultimate league does it.

"All of us go for the glory to a degree," he said. "Too, there's love of country. It's a very proud moment when you've driven a hard-fought race against the best competition in the world and won and you stand at attention as your national anthem is played.

"But the main thing is the driving itself . . . the exhilaration that comes from the control of power and the sense of personal achievement. To come out of a corner at 120 MPH and be able to feed so much power that you have to warp the wheels all the way over in the wrong direction in order to keep going straight. It's a tremendous feeling and it repeats and repeats.

"The element of personal risk in racing adds a special something to the exhilaration, one that you don't find in other sports. That's why high-speed corners are the best. If you go around a hairpin and execute it in a perfect slide it's very nice and you sort of feel that what you did was rather good. But if you go around a really fast corner at 150 or so and you get the car drifting absolutely to perfection and at the absolute,

206

exquisite limit of control — well, that's harder, it's more dangerous, and the feeling of satisfaction when you do it right is tremendous. Doing it right for an entire race is quite an experience to undergo and to look back on."

What does a super-champion do when he hangs up his helmet and goggles? Moss owns a commercial garage and a car-painting business, plus substantial interests in several other enterprises, from a design studio to a launderette chain.

Although he is far too active a type to enjoy reading he likes to write and writes very well. He is the automotive editor of three magazines, is a contributing editor of several others, and is an internationally syndicated newspaper columnist. He also does a great deal of television work. Speaking of all this recently he said, "I'll tell you one thing, Griff, getting a name is fairly difficult, but trying to keep it alive is damn hard work!"

Denis Clive Hulme

1967

"My plan was to lay in fourth place and not to take the slightest chance until I crossed the finish line," Hulme said after his methodical drive at Mexico City. He had needed fourth place to win the 1967 championship and had had third place thrust upon him. Otherwise, he drove the final and decisive race of the season precisely according to schedule.

At the start of the season no one could have been expected to pick Hulme as a promising candidate for the championship. After all, he was just a good piece of supporting talent that had yet to win his first GP race. But, after six long and hard-working years in International racing, Hulme was ready to bloom in full, consistent glory. He was the sole GP driver to score points in nine of the eleven Grandes Epreuves. In the two in which he failed to classify, his Brabham-Repco had stopped running. In all the rest he finished high with machinelike regularity, always matching total determination with cool patience and calm. The first race of the season was his slowest: South Africa, fourth place. After that it was three thirds, three seconds, and two firsts. No one could say that he had lucked into the world title. Hulme earned every one of his 51 points with manifest competence and generalship. He revealed himself as a champion's champion.

Hulme is slow-moving and languid and has an enormous capacity for sleep, which nothing seems to disturb. He is not fond of shoes and likes to drive in his bare feet. He likes cars, trucks, his family, and water sports, and that is the whole sweep of his strong interests in life. He is soft-spoken, not talkative, but very intelligent. He is a country boy from the quiet North Island of New Zealand and it is there that he hopes to retire.

Denis Hulme, the 1967 champion, is typically informal and relaxed as he stands with his boss and teammate Jack Brabham.

He was born in Nelson, New Zealand, on June 18, 1936. His father had him steering the family car before he can remember and he began really to drive when he was six. He loved mechanical work and by the age of ten was making a part-time income as a welder. Except for the sports involved, he found school a complete bore. His father established a small trucking business and Denny became a Diesel mechanic and truck driver. He got his automobile driver's license the day he was fifteen and his truck license at eighteen. He had an appetite for speed.

When he was twenty, in 1957, his parents bought him his first car, an MG TF. He drove it fast on the open road and promptly began competing in hillclimbs, gymkhanas, and drags. Then came the New Zealand GP of 1958, which included a handicap event for MG's. He started at the back of the pack but won.

A few more races confirmed that Denny had real driving talent, and in the winter of 1959 his parents presented him with a new Formula Two Cooper single-seater — one of the best machines in the Islands. He drove this treasure in the New Zealand GP of January, 1960, so impressively that the organizers rewarded him with a driving scholarship to Europe, as they had previously done with Bruce McLaren and would do again with Chris Amon. Denny raced all over Europe that season and, in Formula Junior, was first at Pescara, second at Messina and Salerno, and third on Monza's hallowed ground. Then he returned home, where he won his country's single-seater championship in his 2.5 Cooper-Climax, plus New Zealand's highest racing award, its National Gold Star.

The big time was in Europe, and it was here that Denny promptly returned. Formula Two had been put in hibernation for three years and he had to drive in Formula Junior. The only bright spots of his '61 European season were second places at Pescara and Messina. He decided to stay in Europe and needed work for the winter months. Phil Kerr was an old friend from New Zealand who happened to manage the small commercial garage which Jack Brabham was running. Denny was glad to accept Kerr's offer to do "mechanicking" on passenger cars.

Denny continued to pick up occasional racing rides throughout 1962, but it was not until December of that year that his employer decided to try him in a major Formula Junior race at Brands Hatch. Driving in ice and snow, Denny took the pole position, broke the lap record, and won the Boxing Day race. From that time on he was an official member of the Brabham team.

Success did not come quickly for Hulme in single-seater cars, partly because he was always the second driver, driving according to team instructions. But he was free to let himself go in sports-car racing and it was here that his real brilliance became increasingly clear.

Driving second to Brabham in 1966, Denny had bad mechanical luck; yet, to his delighted surprise, finished the season with a very honorable eighteen championship points.

Then came 1967 and the opening race in South Africa, which he immediately realized he could have won. In the second race, Monaco, he made up his mind to try to win it, and did. Then he knew that he was on his way and that nothing had to stand between him and the championship, and it did not.

"The best thing about racing," Denis Hulme says, "is what it can do for a man in terms of discovering himself. It is hard to know when you are at your best. Racing can permit you to find this out."

III

Appendices

Appendix A

Formula One in the Championship Era

1947 — 1953   Piston displacement limited to 1500 cc (91.5 cubic inch) supercharged, 4500 cc (274 cubic inch) unsupercharged. No restrictions on fuel or on vehicle weight.

1954 — 1960   Piston displacement limited to 2500 cc (152 cubic inch) unsupercharged and 750 cc (45 cubic inch) supercharged. (No 750 cc Formula One cars were built.) No restriction on vehicle weight. No restriction on fuel until 1958, when "commercial gasoline" became mandatory.

1961 — 1965   Piston displacement limited to 1500 cc (91.5 cubic inch) maximum and 1300 cc (79 cubic inch) minimum. Supercharging prohibited. Minimum vehicle weight of 450 kilograms (990 pounds), with water and oil but without fuel. Commercial gasoline only. In the interest of safety, self-starter, two independent braking systems, safety belt, safety-type fuel tanks, open cockpit, and open wheels. Replenishment of oil prohibited during the course of any race.

1966 — 1970   Piston displacement limited to 3000 cc (183 cubic inch) unsupercharged, 1500 cc (91.5 cubic inch) supercharged. Minimum vehicle weight of 500 kilograms (1100 pounds), with water and oil but without fuel. Commercial gasoline only.

Appendix B
The World Championship
of Drivers

Inaugurated in 1950

YEAR	DRIVER	NATION-ALITY	POINTS	CAR	NATION-ALITY
1950	GIUSEPPE FARINA	ITAL	30	ALFA ROMEO	ITAL
	J. M. Fangio	ARG	27	Alfa Romeo	ITAL
	Luigi Fagioli	ITAL	24	Alfa Romeo	ITAL
1951	J. M. FANGIO	ARG	31	ALFA ROMEO	ITAL
	Alberto Ascari	ITAL	25	Ferrari	ITAL
	Froilan Gonzales	ARG	24	Ferrari	ITAL
1952	ALBERTO ASCARI	ITAL	36	FERRARI	ITAL
	Giuseppe Farina	ITAL	24	Ferrari	ITAL
	Piero Taruffi	ITAL	22	Ferrari	ITAL
1953	ALBERTO ASCARI	ITAL	34.5	FERRARI	ITAL
	J. M. Fangio	ARG	28	Maserati	ITAL
	Giuseppe Farina	ITAL	26	Ferrari	ITAL
1954	J. M. FANGIO	ARG	42	MASERATI	ITAL
				MERCEDES-BENZ	GER
	Froilan Gonzales	ARG	25.14	Ferrari	ITAL
	Mike Hawthorn	ENG	24.64	Ferrari	ITAL
1955	J. M. FANGIO	ARG	40	MERCEDES-BENZ	GER
	Stirling Moss	ENG	23	Mercedes-Benz	GER
	Eugenio Castelotti	ITAL	12	Ferrari	ITAL
1956	J. M. FANGIO	ARG	30	LANCIA/-	ITAL
				FERRARI	
	Stirling Moss	ENG	27	Maserati	ITAL
	Peter Collins	ENG	25	Lancia/Ferrari	ITAL
1957	J. M. FANGIO	ARG	40	MASERATI	ITAL
	Stirling Moss	ENG	25	Vanwall	ENG
	Luigi Musso	ITAL	16	Lancia/Ferrari	ITAL
1958	MIKE HAWTHORN	ENG	42	FERRARI	ITAL
	Stirling Moss	ENG	41	Cooper, Vanwall	ENG
	Tony Brooks	ENG	24	Vanwall	ENG

YEAR	DRIVER	NATION-ALITY	POINTS	CAR	NATION-ALITY
1959	JACK BRABHAM	AUS	31	COOPER	ENG
	Tony Brooks	ENG	27	Ferrari	ITAL
	Stirling Moss	ENG	25.5	Cooper, BRM	ENG
1960	JACK BRABHAM	AUS	43	COOPER	ENG
	Bruce McLaren	ENG	34	Cooper	ENG
	Stirling Moss	ENG	19	Lotus	ENG
1961	PHIL HILL	USA	34	FERRARI	ITAL
	Wolfgang von Trips	GER	33	Ferrari	ITAL
	Stirling Moss	ENG	21	Lotus	ENG
	Dan Gurney	USA	21	Porsche	GER
1962	GRAHAM HILL	ENG	42	BRM	ENG
	Jim Clark	SCOT	30	Lotus	ENG
	Bruce McLaren	ENG	27	Cooper	ENG
1963	JIM CLARK	SCOT	54	LOTUS	ENG
	Graham Hill	ENG	29	BRM	ENG
	Richie Ginther	USA	28	BRM	ENG
1964	JOHN SURTEES	ENG	41	FERRARI	ITAL
	Graham Hill	ENG	39	BRM	ENG
	Jim Clark	ENG	32	Lotus	ENG
1965	JIM CLARK	SCOT	54	LOTUS	ENG
	Graham Hill	ENG	40	BRM	ENG
	Jackie Stewart	ENG	33	BRM	ENG
1966	JACK BRABHAM	AUS	45	BRABHAM-REPCO	ENG
	John Surtees	ENG	28	Ferrari	ITAL
				Cooper-Maserati	ENG-ITAL
	Jochen Rindt	SWITZ	22	Cooper-Climax	ENG
1967	DENIS HULME	NZ	51	BRABHAM-REPCO	ENG
	Jack Brabham	AUS	46	Brabham-Repco	ENG
	Jim Clark	SCOT	41	Lotus-Ford	ENG

Appendix C

The Manufacturers' Championship

This category was created by the FIA in 1958 and was dropped at the end of the 1967 season. The scoring system is similar to that of the World Championship of Drivers. Only the leading car of each make receives points. Final, net points are based on best five placings.

YEAR	MAKE	POINTS	NATIONALITY
1958	Vanwall	48	British
	Ferrari	40	Italian
	Cooper	31	British
1959	Cooper	40	British
	Ferrari	32	Italian
	BRM	19	British
1960	Cooper	40	British
	Lotus	32	British
	Ferrari	24	Italian
1961	Ferrari	40	Italian
	Lotus	32	British
	Porsche	22	German
1962	BRM	42	British
	Lotus	36	British
	Cooper	29	British
1963	Lotus	54	British
	BRM	36	British
	Brabham	28	British

1964	Ferrari	45	Italian
	BRM	42	British
	Lotus	38	British
1965	Lotus	54	British
	BRM	45	British
	Brabham	27	British
1966	Brabham-Repco	42	British-Australian-USA
	Ferrari	31	Italian
	Cooper-Maserati	30	British-Italian
1967	Brabham-Repco	63	British-Australian
	Lotus-Ford	44	British
	Cooper-Maserati	28	British-Italian

Index

Figures in italics denote illustrations

220

Index

221

Index

Index

Index

Index

225

Index

About the Author

Griffith Borgeson was born in California and attended the University of California at Berkeley. He is the author of *The Golden Age of the American Racing Car*, and recipient of the 1967 Thomas McKeon Memorial Cup, given annually by the Antique Automobile Club of America for excellence in automotive historical research.

Mr. Borgeson and his wife live in France.